In celebration of wisdom

Occasional Papers, no. 26
Institute of Mennonite Studies

Occasional Papers are occasional publications of the Institute of Mennonite Studies at Associated Mennonite Biblical Seminary, Elkhart, Indiana. IMS was founded in 1958 to promote and create opportunities for research, conversation, and publication on topics and issues vital to Mennonite congregations and the Anabaptist faith tradition.

In the Occasional Papers series, IMS—sometimes in collaboration with other Mennonite publishers—publishes essays in the fields of Bible, history, theology, ethics, and pastoral ministry. The intent of the series is to foster discussion and to seek counsel, particularly from within the Mennonite theological community. Many essays are in finished form; some may be in a more germinal stage, released for purposes of testing and inviting critical response.

In accepting papers for publication, IMS gives priority to authors (faculty, students, alumni) from Mennonite seminaries, colleges, and universities.

In celebration of wisdom

Life and meaning in Job, Proverbs, and Ecclesiastes

edited by Steven Schweitzer

Occasional Papers, no. 26

Institute of Mennonite Studies
Elkhart, Indiana

WIPF & STOCK · Eugene, Oregon

Wipf and Stock Publishers
199 W 8th Ave, Suite 3
Eugene, OR 97401

In Celebration of Wisdom
Life and Meaning in Job, Proverbs, and Ecclesiastes
By Schweitzer, Steven
Copyright©2009 Institute of Mennonite Studies
ISBN 13: 978-1-5326-3159-7
Publication date 4/21/2017
Previously published by Institute of Mennonite Studies, 2009

Unless otherwise indicated, the scripture quotations in this book are from the New Revised Standard Version of the Bible, copyright © 1989 by the Division of Christian Education of the National Council of Churches of Christ in the USA, and are used by permission.

Contents

	Introduction *Steven Schweitzer*	1
1	**Metaphors and meaning in Proverbs 5:15–20** *Jesse Smith*	9
2	**A reader-response critical assessment of Proverbs 6:20–35** *V. EuGene Kennard*	15
3	**Reclaiming the woman of substance: Proverbs 31:10–31** *Jenifer Eriksen-Morales*	21
4	**Who is this wisdom to whom we sing? Job 28** *Samuel Voth Schrag*	27
5	**Job's legal defense: Job 31** *Renee Kanagy*	33
6	**Laying the foundations: God's appearance in Job 38–39** *Tommy Boutell*	39
7	**Animals and humanity in the world: Job 38–39** *Brianne Donaldson*	45
8	**Flinging ourselves upon the impossible: Job 38–39 and human suffering through the eyes of liberation theology** *Elizabeth Miller*	51
9	**Relinquishing illusions, finding joy: Ecclesiastes 11.1–8** *Gloria Beck*	57
10	**Because God is your share in life: A reading of Ecclesiastes 9:7–12** *Suella Gerber*	61
11	**Paradoxes and contradictions in Ecclesiastes 7:1–18** *Sylvie Gudin*	67
12	**Living life in the present: Ecclesiastes 9:7–12** *Jill Schreiber*	73
13	**An Easter message? Ecclesiastes 9:7–12** *Rachel Siemens*	79

Introduction

Steven Schweitzer

The thirteen essays in this volume engage biblical texts from the three books in the Hebrew Bible associated with the wisdom tradition in ancient Israel: Proverbs, Job, and Ecclesiastes. These three books provide deep theological reflection on everyday life and practical ethics. Often ignored in the development of theology, in favor of concepts such as covenant or the foundational teachings in the Torah (Law), these books contain a richness and usefulness the church—especially the North American church—desperately needs to hear in our contemporary cultural contexts. These essays affirm the value of these books, not just for understanding Israel's ideas about wisdom, or even Israel's ideas about faith, but also for the continuing theological witness and development of the church.[1]

Historically, the Israelite wisdom tradition has much in common with wisdom traditions of other ancient Near Eastern cultures, especially those of Sumer, Babylon, and Egypt. These older traditions from surrounding cultures deal with issues raised in Israel's wisdom texts, ranging from understandings of theodicy and the problem of evil, to practical advice on how to live as an effective member of society, to consideration of how to shape a coherent

---

Steven Schweitzer is assistant professor of Old Testament at Associated Mennonite Biblical Seminary. He regularly teaches courses on Job and Wisdom, Psalms, Chronicles-Ezra-Nehemiah, and Second Temple Judaism. He also teaches Sunday school and preaches in his home congregation, Prince of Peace Church of the Brethren, in South Bend, Indiana.

[1] This introduction provides only the briefest introduction to Wisdom literature. For an excellent book-length introduction, see especially Richard Clifford, *The Wisdom Literature* (Nashville: Abingdon Press, 1998); James Crenshaw, *Old Testament Wisdom: An Introduction* (Louisville: Westminster John Knox Press, 1998); Katharine Dell, *"Get Wisdom, Get Insight": An Introduction to Israel's Wisdom Literature* (Macon, GA: Smyth & Helwys Publishing, 2000); and Tremper Longman III and Peter Enns, eds., *Dictionary of the Old Testament: Wisdom, Poetry and Writings* (Downers Grove, IL: InterVarsity Press, 2008).

worldview. So for example, the books of Job and Ecclesiastes have precedents in such texts as "Dialogue between a Man and his God," "The Poem of the Righteous Sufferer," "The Babylonian Theodicy," and "The Dialogue on Pessimism." The book of Proverbs contains many sayings that appear in a wide range of texts throughout the ancient Near East. Worthy of note is the adaptation in Proverbs 22:17–24:22 of traditions found in the thirteenth-century BCE Egyptian *Instructions of Amenemope*. Here we see Israelite sages recognizing the existence of truth outside Israel's heritage, finding it in Egyptian materials, and bringing those ideas into the Israelite faith tradition.

These connections illustrate the universal nature of the wisdom tradition. Many ideas and statements about the cosmos found in Israel's Wisdom literature are echoed in the wisdom literature of other cultures. Further the Israelite wisdom books pay scant attention to uniquely Israelite concerns such as the Torah, the covenant, and figures of Israel's past (Abraham, Moses, or David, for example). Other important institutions—the monarchy, the priesthood, the temple and its sacrificial system, and prophecy—are marginalized, if not completely ignored. Wisdom also conveys a perspective that transcends time and space; it is atemporal and often ahistorical, applicable to all humanity regardless of cultural and religious background. It exemplifies general rather than specific revelation. Many scholars have understood the wisdom books as a countervoice, an alternative Israelite theological tradition. Perhaps it is best to see the movement responsible for these ideas as one voice among many in an ensemble. We (and the majority of Jews and Christians over the centuries) have given priority to the Torah or the Prophetic Books but pushed Wisdom literature to the side. From the margin, wisdom has scarcely been allowed to speak, although it has much to say.

Wisdom (*hokmah* in Hebrew, *sophia* in Greek) emphasizes an epistemology (how we know what we know) anchored in empirical observation. The wise person is counseled to look at the surrounding world to discern the principles that control reality. Wisdom theology emphasizes the creative activity of God. In creating the universe, God put in place principles that bring order instead of chaos to life, harmony instead of discord, and regularity instead of randomness. The sages, according to the wisdom tradition, aspire to bring their lives in line with the principles at work in God's creation, to discern God's order and purposes, and to live in accordance with these established values. To live apart from God's inherent system is to be a fool. Essentially, humans can observe the natural world and come to understand God's wisdom, God's way for humanity to live productively in this world. Several important convictions follow from this basic stance: wisdom is accessible and knowable rather than hidden and endlessly elusive; wisdom is pervasive, touching all aspects of existence; and wisdom values experience as a means of understanding the divine. Human experience—all experience in this world—is material that can be used to develop theology. God is not restricted to the Torah or the prophetic voice. God can be approached through nature, through creation, through experience.

The relationship between hokmah (wisdom) and shalom (God's holistic ordered reality, often translated "peace") is worth pondering. Hokmah is one way of achieving shalom; in fact, shalom is impossible without hokmah. In many respects, the two terms are synonyms: God's wisdom echoes God's shalom, and God's shalom reflects God's wisdom. To live the good life is to live according to the principles of shalom and the principles of wisdom; the two are inseparable.

This parallel between wisdom and peaceful existence (shalom) can also be identified in Egyptian wisdom literature's concept of Ma'at—the word for both the goddess of wisdom and the manifestation of that divine attribute. In Egyptian wisdom traditions, Ma'at is the fundamental principle that provides order, justice, truth, and reason in the universe. Pharaoh claims to do Ma'at, to eat or live on Ma'at, and to promote Ma'at in this world. The Pharaoh's life will be judged on the basis of Ma'at. In the Egyptian funerary texts, the solar barque of Re is guided by the figure of Ma'at at the boat's bow.[2] In *The Book of the Dead*, the heart of Pharaoh is weighed on the scales of justice against the feather of Ma'at, the feather being the traditional symbol of the goddess. If Pharaoh has balanced the scales in line with Ma'at, then he will be welcomed into the next world. If not, Pharaoh's heart will be consumed by Anubis, the jackal. The

---

[2] See the Pyramid Texts, spells or utterances found in the tombs of the Pharaohs of the fifth and sixth dynasties, dating to circa 2300 BCE. They are some of the oldest written Egyptian texts.

scribal god Toth stands ready to record the verdict.³ Thus, Ma'at is the standard by which one's life, or at least the lives of the social elite, may be judged.⁴

Israel's wisdom tradition echoes these ideas, though without references to Egyptian deities. This is particularly noticeable in Proverbs 8:22-31, which describes the relationship of God and Hokmah (Wisdom) in terms reminiscent of the goddess Ma'at. Undoubtedly, Egyptian ideas about Ma'at influenced Israelite understandings of judgment, wisdom, creation, justice, and shalom. As the church refines its theology on similar topics, some knowledge of the Egyptian concepts that fueled the formation of Israel's theological views could assist us in our endeavors. Too often the church has failed to recognize the importance of comparative studies, which provide a helpful way to understand what the authors of the Bible were actually saying and how they saw their relationship to the surrounding cultural and philosophical systems of their day.

So, what is wisdom? Having laid out some of the key issues, I can now try to answer that question. Wisdom is how to live life. It is practical and ethical; it consists of principles that guide decision making; and it helps us align ourselves with God's order. But wisdom cannot be reduced to simple axioms that are unvaryingly true. In Proverbs 26:4-5, for example, the reader is told first, "Do not answer fools according to their folly, or you will be a fool yourself," and then, "Answer fools according to their folly, or they will be wise in their own eyes." So which is it? Should we speak or keep our mouths shut? Notice that both pieces of apparently contradictory advice are given—back to back—as flat commands, without qualification or nuance. How can both be true? But that is the point: both *are* true, and wisdom—true wisdom—is knowing which situation calls for us to speak and which situation requires us to be silent. Wisdom is knowing what to do in a particular situation, when to apply which

---

³ Note the connection between the Egyptian wisdom tradition and scribes. A similar association between sages and scribes is apparent in the Israelite tradition.

⁴ In later texts, it is not only Pharaoh but also his immediate circle of advisors and individuals of high social status who may "do Ma'at" and thus gain a blessed afterlife. However, this access is never extended to the majority of the population. In this respect, the democratization of wisdom—accessibility beyond the king and the royal court—is a development within the Israelite wisdom tradition.

advice; wisdom is being aware and knowledgeable in order to make the right decision based on all information available. Hence, wisdom affirms the importance of empirical observation, of actually opening our eyes and seeing the world around us.

Wisdom literature, especially Job and Ecclesiastes, may be the most useful biblical books for the church in our postmodern climate.[5] As the church tries to articulate its theology and ethics in the midst of shifting cultural philosophies, the Old Testament Wisdom literature provides us not just with counsel about how to live but with a model for how to construct theology creatively and authentically. Rather than withdraw from society and culture, the church must engage them productively, embracing what is good and building on it while undertaking a critique of what is deficient. Wisdom literature has the power and perspective the church needs in its present struggle to find its way in the wake of modernism and with the rise of postmodernism. How can the church value its tradition while creating space for innovation? How can the church affirm pluralities instead of monisms as we articulates our theology? Modernism's certainty often conflicts with postmodernism's ambiguity, but both can be brought into dialogue if we follow the pattern set forth by Wisdom literature. The church needs biblical paradigms for navigating complex issues, and the wisdom tradition is an untapped resource in our efforts. We would do well to return to these books, ponder them, and learn from them as we too ask questions about life, meaning, ethics, belief, and living without resolving all the tensions that permeate our existence. In essence, Wisdom literature echoes many immediate concerns for the church. We should not neglect the great gift that has come down to us in the form of wisdom.

The thirteen essays in this collection represent recent attempts to join in this theological enterprise. All were originally oral presentations based on research papers and delivered during the

---

[5] A few recent books echo my claim, although I would not agree with all of their assessments and conclusions: James Limburg, *Encountering Ecclesiastes: A Book for Our Time* (Grand Rapids: Eerdmans, 2006); Donn Morgan, *The Making of Sages: Biblical Wisdom and Contemporary Culture* (Harrisburg, PA: Trinity Press International, 2002); Leo Perdue, *The Sword and the Stylus: An Introduction to Wisdom in the Age of Empires* (Grand Rapids: Eerdmans, 2008); and T. Anthony Perry, *God's Twilight Zone: Wisdom in the Hebrew Bible* (Peabody, MA: Hendrickson Publishers, 2008).

spring 2007 semester by the Master of Arts and Master of Divinity students in the Job and Wisdom Literature course at Associated Mennonite Biblical Seminary. They retain the character of oral compositions and have not been significantly modified, apart from the addition of footnotes. These papers engage texts from the books of Proverbs, Job, and Ecclesiastes (also known by its Hebrew name, Qoheleth), using a variety of methods and with a variety of intended outcomes. Some students approached the text historically; some, literarily; some, philosophically; others, theologically; and still others, homiletically. All treat the biblical text with respect and appropriate academic rigor in their quests to discover something more about wisdom. Each essay is inspirational. Each calls us back to the biblical text, to think through it once more, to see something new or to ask new questions, to read carefully and thoughtfully, to hear ancient voices and consider what they may say to us. All of us in the course were challenged and encouraged by these brief assessments of biblical Wisdom literature.

Three essays examine the book of Proverbs. First, Jesse Smith explores possible layers of meaning in the water imagery used to convey truth about how this world functions ("Metaphors and meaning in Proverbs 5:15–20"). In this passage, both literal and metaphorical meanings illuminate complex social and family relationships. Second, Gene Kennard offers a literary approach to the advice found in Proverbs 6 ("A reader-response critical assessment of Proverbs 6:20–35"). Using a reader-response method focused on the ancient audience, Kennard situates the advice of the passage within a plausible context to answer such questions as: Who heard this advice? How is the argument convincing? and What is the source for the text's persuasive power? Third, Jenifer Eriksen Morales, in "Reclaiming the woman of substance: Proverbs 31:10–31," examines the presentation of the woman in Proverbs 31, which has been a source of joy and pain for women through the centuries. The essay moves from a focus on the actions of this woman to an appreciation of the woman's connection to the principles valued in the wisdom tradition.

The second group of essays probes the book of Job. In his reflections on Job 28, "Who is this wisdom to whom we sing?" Samuel Voth Schrag discusses this poem which serves as a hymn in praise of wisdom. The chapter reveals insights into the nature of God and

God's relationship with humanity, and it may be one key to knowing how best to read the book of Job as a whole. In the next essay, "Job's legal defense," Renee Kanagy examines the legal metaphors that permeate the book of Job, with particular attention to the oath found in Job 31. In his desire to present his case to God, Job uses the strongest language of his time. Job discovers that his understanding of God—the traditional view—cannot hold.

Next come three essays on Job 38-39. In the first, "Laying the foundations: God's appearance in Job 38-39," Tommy Boutell evaluates the portrayal of the divine in the God speeches in these chapters. The image of God rejects simple answers and affirms divine mystery beyond humanity's ability to comprehend. This is the appropriate foundation for doing theology. Next, Brianne Donaldson ("Animals and humanity in the world") carefully considers the provocative relationship between humanity and the animal kingdom in the God speeches. The value placed on animals by the Creator is manifested in a set of ethical and theological claims different from the ones normally espoused by those focused on the divine-human relationship in the book. In "Flinging ourselves upon the impossible: Job 38-39 and innocent suffering through the eyes of liberation theology," Elizabeth Miller builds on the work of Gustavo Gutiérrez in placing Job within the framework of liberation theology. The concern for social injustice and the plight of the poor are central issues in the book, which merits attention from theologians and churches seeking to articulate a Christian response to the tragedy of suffering.

The final group of essays engages the underappreciated book of Ecclesiastes. These five writers find hope, optimism, and resources for living our lives in this world in the words of Qoheleth, who is often viewed as a pessimist. First, Gloria Beck ("Relinquishing illusions, finding joy: Ecclesiastes 11:1-8") offers an inspiring address on the value of not knowing, which appears in the book's acute emphasis on humanity's inability to comprehend the complexities of life. It is in recognizing and embracing our inability to know that we find hope and meaning in simplicity and in living an active life. Second, Suella Gerber ("Because God is your share in life") offers the first of three treatments of Ecclesiastes 9:7-12. In this short text, the author encourages readers to embrace the joy that can be found in life, even in the midst of mystery and struggle. The outlook of this text is not pessimistic but instead celebrates the advantages of placing God at the center of our lives. Third, Sylvie Gudin ("Paradoxes and contradictions in Ecclesiastes 7:1–18") places the "absurdity" of Ecclesiastes in conversation with the philosophy of the absurd articulated by Albert Camus. The fleeting existence of humans and the advice to enjoy life while it lasts are viewed as expressions of realism and pragmatism that shape our existence in this world.

The final two essays approach Ecclesiastes 9:7–12 from different perspectives. In "Living life in the present," Jill Schreiber provides a close reading of the movement of language in this passage, which brings together despair and hope, acknowledging the pain of the present while holding out an ethic that moves us into living in the midst of our present circumstances. In the final essay, "An Easter message?" Rachel Siemens explores how the language used in this passage echoes common Easter motifs, which celebrate the mystery and wonder of life through images of hope in the midst of difficult times.

These students read astutely and with passion. We hope their essays will bring you wisdom, as they inspired us when they were first voiced. I wish to thank the Institute of Mennonite Studies at Associated Mennonite Biblical Seminary, especially Barbara Nelson Gingerich for her exemplary editorial work, and Herald Press for copublishing them. Our hope is that these reflections will inspire those who read them to return to biblical Wisdom literature to seek wisdom, to gain insight, to pursue what is elusive, and to revel in the joy that God gives throughout life's mysterious journey, to all of us who are but strangers and pilgrims in this transient yet beautiful world.[6]

---

[6] See Eccles. 3.

Chapter 1

Metaphors and meaning in Proverbs 5:15-20

Jesse Smith

Proverbs 1-9 records the lessons an unnamed sage shares with his "son" (student). The teaching in chapter five can be divided into two contrasting sections: the first (5:3-14) exhorts the young man to avoid the strange woman:

> ³For the lips of a loose woman drip honey,
>   and her speech is smoother than oil;
> ⁴but in the end she is bitter as wormwood,
>   sharp as a two-edged sword.
> ⁵Her feet go down to death;
>   her steps follow the path to Sheol.
> ⁶She does not keep straight to the path of life;
>   her ways wander, and she does not know it.
>   (Prov. 5:3-6)

The concluding admonition (vv. 15-20) punctuates the preceding instruction by shifting away from the foreign woman to one's own wife.

> ¹⁵Drink water from your own cistern,
>   flowing water from your own well.
> ¹⁶Should your springs be scattered abroad,
>   streams of water in the streets?
> ¹⁷Let them be for yourself alone,
>   and not for sharing with strangers.
> ¹⁸Let your fountain be blessed,
>   and rejoice in the wife of your youth,
>   a lovely deer, a graceful doe.
> ¹⁹May her breasts satisfy you at all times;
>   may you be intoxicated always by her love.

Jesse Smith is a second-year student in the Master of Divinity program at Associated Mennonite Biblical Seminary. He is a 2006 graduate of Goshen College and comes from Iowa City, Iowa.

> ²⁰Why should you be intoxicated, my son, by another woman and embrace the bosom of an adulteress?

In these later verses, the sage alters not just his tone—negative to positive—but also his rhetorical devices. In verses 15-18, the teacher employs allegory, "understood as an extension of the comparative element into a whole series of concrete sayings."[1] Water images become allegories for sexual intimacy between a husband and wife. But the imagery in verses 15-18 brings with it what one commentator calls "problems of interpretation, ambiguity, and obscurity."[2]

In attempting to grapple with this exegetical uncertainty, this essay first offers general notes on the interpretation of verses 15 and 16. Delving deeper into the imagery, it next describes two possible readings of the text. In conclusion, it suggests those aspects of the two interpretations that ring true, and incorporates the passage into the larger framework of Proverbs.

Monogamy

In his commentary on Proverbs, William McKane correctly states that "there is nothing contentious about v. 15: 'Drink water from your own cistern, the streams which flow from your own well' means 'have sexual intercourse only with your wife.'"[3] This understanding is most easily gathered from the verses directly following the allegory. In verses 18-20, the sage breaks the suspense his imagery has created and reveals the subject under discussion: the young wife. Faithfulness to one's wife is clearly the instruction given in verse 15. But we must ask, why does the sage encourage monogamy? (Conversely, we might ask why the sage prohibits sexual licentiousness.) Verse 16 is crucial to answering this question. However, as William McKane notes, verse 16 has not been interpreted consistently:

> In v. 16, if the LXX [the Greek version of the Old Testament] is followed, the translation is either: (a) 'lest (inserting *pen*) your springs be dispersed outside, channels of water in the

---

[1] Philip Johannes Nel, *The Structure and Ethos of the Wisdom Admonitions in Proverbs* (Berlin: Walter de Gruyter, 1982), 10.
[2] William McKane, *Proverbs: A New Approach,* Old Testament Library (Philadelphia: Westminster Press, 1970), 318.
[3] Ibid.

streets' (Gemser), or (b) 'Let not (inserting *'al*) your springs be dispersed outside, channels of water in the street.' If MT (Masoretic Text [the standard Hebrew text]) is read, the translation is either: (a) 'Should your springs be dispersed outside, channels of water in the streets?' (Toy), or (b): '(and so) your springs will be dispersed outside channels of water in the streets.'[4]

Moving forward, I suggest two possible interpretations of the larger passage that emerge as a result of different readings of verse 16.

Fertility

If one reads verses 15–16 as "Drink water from your own cistern, flowing water from your own well, (and so) your springs be scattered abroad, streams of water in the street," the cistern becomes an image of fertility. "Numerous progeny will be given to the man who reserves all his virility for his wife (v. 17). The overflowing wells represent a gift of abundant prosperity."[5] One's offspring (the stream) will fill the street and the square.

Monogamy makes possible this result. "The wife is a receptacle for her husband's 'water' that will yield offspring. In a land where water was scarce, where cisterns were built to store every drop for the sake of irrigation and survival, the image makes a strong equation between marital infidelity on the parts of the husband and wife and the wastage of precious natural resources."[6] Fill your own well (wife), and your water (offspring) will overflow into the streets. Waste your virility by filling another, and you waste a precious resource. How precious?

> Ancient Israel, like many ancient agricultural societies, depended heavily on families having lots of children. Analyses of remains in Israel and similar societies indicate that only a minority of live births survived into the second year.... Women tended to die about ten years earlier than men, often during childbirth or as the result of complications attending frequent pregnancy. Within this context, every fertile woman needed to produce more than five live births during

---

[4] Ibid.
[5] Ibid.
[6] Milton P. Horne *Proverbs*, Smith & Helwys Bible Commentary (Macon, GA: Smith & Helwys Publishing, 2003), 96.

her adult life in order for the next generation to take the current generation's place.... Thus the reproductive potential of fertile women was highly valued.[7]

The wise would certainly be concerned with producing offspring. But is fertility the primary reason to encourage monogamy in 5:15-20? Is procreation the theme? Probably not. Children are indeed a blessing, but they are not mentioned. Nor are classical metaphors for fertility. What is more, the sage does not present his pupil with a contrast between a barren foreign woman and a fertile wife. Both are able to produce offspring.

Society

If one interprets verses 15-16 to read, "Drink water from your own cistern, flowing water from your own well; *let not* your springs be scattered abroad, streams of water in the street," a very different meaning comes into focus. The sage warns against adultery because it is a disruptive force in society. (The same interpretation might also be achieved by treating v. 17 as an answer to the rhetorical question posed in v. 16: "Should your springs be scattered abroad, streams of water in the street? Let them be for yourself alone, and not for sharing with strangers.") William McKane notes that "the cistern is for collecting rain water, and the overflow from the well, which may be fed by underground springs, must be stored in a cistern and not allowed to run waste into the streets."[8] If precious water leaks into the streets, the family and ultimately society itself are threatened. Here, streams in the streets represent disaster or chaos. Something is wrong, not right, when water is in the streets. Boundaries are washed away and resources wasted.

Adultery was intolerable in ancient Israel because it threatened the social structure, which depended on the stability of the family.[9] "Moreover," writes Michael Fox, "promiscuity throws patrimony into uncertainty, denying a man confidence that his heirs are his own offspring.... Women received the seed and bore children to inherit the land. As a result, many Biblical traditions aim to en-

---

[7] David M. Carr, *The Erotic World: Sexuality, Spirituality and the Bible* (New York: Oxford University Press, 2003), 49-50.
[8] McKane, *Proverbs*, 318.
[9] Michel V. Fox, *Proverbs 1-9: A New Translation with Introduction and Commentary* (New York: Doubleday, 2000), 208.

sure that proper women became vessels of Israelite seed."[10] If this text originates from the early part of the Persian period, as many scholars believe, concern for Israelite stability would have been amplified. The seduction of foreign culture and foreign women threatened Jewish identity and Jewish society. "The sages, including the one who uttered this wisdom, sought to shape a Jewish society that would survive into the future."[11]

Conclusion: Wisdom

While a preoccupation with fertility may be the focus of a questionable interpretation of 5:15–20, there are certainly societal concerns at work here. (Some have even suggested that this passage deals with economic concerns related to the dowry). Yet we have noticed that this text is explicit in describing the personal joys monogamy brings. The lecture does not merely "concede the legitimacy of conjugal relations, along the lines of 'better to marry than to burn' (some of the medieval commentators read it this way)."[12] Michael Fox calls this "the only passage in the Bible that celebrates the pleasures of marital sex, with the partial exception of the Song of Songs. . . . It addresses the male reader and positively encourages him to take his fill of legitimate erotic pleasures."[13]

By placing this description of pleasure after a warning against temptation, the author acknowledges the difficulty of monogamy. But its reward is clear. There is richness in fidelity. "Sex, within the context of marriage, is one of the fruits of the 'good life' (v. 15)."[14] And the good life is a product of wisdom. Here, as in much of Proverbs, wise decisions lead to reward. Union with one's wife (or Woman Wisdom) leads to "intoxicating love." Coupling with the adulteress (or Woman Folly) leads to Sheol, the place of the dead.

Thus this passage presents a complex view of sexual relationships. Adultery is viewed as a folly of individual men and women that harms those who commit it. Monogamy is described as bringing joy to the individual. However, some communal understanding of sex is certainly at work. The passage moves from a place as public

---

[10] Ibid.
[11] Carr, *Erotic World*, 50.
[12] Fox, *Proverbs 1-9*, 207.
[13] Ibid.
[14] Dermot Cox, *Proverbs, with an Introduction to Sapiential Books,* Old Testament Message 17 (Wilmington, DE: Michael Glazier, 1982), 136.

as the streets to a place as intimate as a spouse's breasts. Sex, in all its complexities and beauty, is brought into the light. But it was never hidden from God: "For human ways are under the eyes of the Lord, and he examines all their paths" (v. 21).

Chapter 2

A reader-response critical assessment of Proverbs 6:20–35

V. EuGene Kennard

Proverbs 6:20–35 places a young man squarely in the trajectory of proverbial commands and implications. These verses instruct "my child"—evidently a son—according to the law of God; they are to be identified by the reader/responder with principles that are non-negotiable.[1] These proverbs demand righteousness and purity, and the obedient son who follows them will experience a lifetime of faithfulness.

In Proverbs 6:20-25 the reader/responder would find parallels with familiar teachings he has received through studying the Torah. By implementing the reader-response critical method of study, we can also discover such parallels. We find good examples in Deuteronomy 6:2–3, 24–25. Here, as elsewhere in the Torah, we learn that one generation is to pass on to the next the teaching of the commandments and statutes.

The reader is instructed to observe the commandments of his father, and not to forsake the teaching of his mother. These proverbs assume that the parents' commandments and teachings will be in agreement with the law of God.[2] Were they not to be, the reader would be required to follow a higher authority. He would not be compelled to break the holy law. If his parents strayed

---

V. EuGene Kennard holds a BA in pastoral theology from Trinity Baptist College in Jacksonville, Florida, and a Master of Arts in Theological Studies from Associated Mennonite Biblical Seminary. He and his wife, Deborah, work for a Christian youth and family service, where they minister to boys and girls in need of direction and love.

[1] For a brief introduction to and demonstration of reader-response criticism, see Edgar V. McKnight, "Reader-Response Criticism," in *To Each Its Own Meaning: An Introduction to Biblical Criticisms and Their Application*, ed. Stephen R. Haynes and Steven L. McKenzie, rev. ed. (Louisville: Westminster John Knox Press, 1999), 230–52.

[2] George Lawson, *Proverbs: Timeless Truths for Practical Living* (Grand Rapids: Kregel Publications, 1980), 120.

from the truthful principles of God, his parents would become his enemies.[3]

These verses command the son to bind these words of instruction on his heart, and to tie them around his neck. This figurative language portrays a young person who embraces sound teaching and saturates himself with instruction. As he walks about, the light of the law will guide his path. When he sleeps, he will be protected. When he is awake, the instructions of his godly parents will continuously instruct him and teach him the way he should walk in. Apparently this young man will soon make decisions on his own; he may already be in the practice of doing so. "Discipline, though painful, helps keep a person on the right path, leading him in the way of life."[4]

While many temptations await a young man, the centerpiece of his parents' counsel is to be wary of the seductive and adulterous woman.[5] This warning indicates that the young man has reached an age of sexual awareness, and that the timing of his parents' instructions coincides with the real-life drama the young man is already experiencing. It also indicates that parents have long been in the practice of giving their sons advice and warnings.

The young reader is told that the evil woman will have a smooth tongue and flattering lips (vv. 24–25). As the young man reads the proverb, and recognizes the quality of his parents' teachings, he can readily identify the natural urges and temptations he has already been facing. The wisdom writings serve as a backdrop to all he has been learning.

These proverbs give the young man practical and potentially life-saving advice. The text acknowledges that the evil woman can be, and probably will be, beautiful. Her flirting eyes, her other at-

---

[3] Ibid.
[4] John H. Walvoord and Roy B. Zuck, *The Bible Knowledge Commentary* (Wheaton, IL: Victor Books, 1988), 917.
[5] This depiction of the dangerous woman is problematic. While this statement is not a comment on all women, the text is open to misogynist and abusive interpretations. My intention is not to engage in a feminist reading or one that attempts to rehabilitate an oppressive text constructed in a very different context, one governed by patriarchy. My essay aims at understanding that ancient context through rhetorical criticism. For an excellent approach to issues of gender in this text, see Claudia V. Camp, *Wise, Strange, and Holy: The Strange Woman and the Making of the Bible*, Journal for the Study of the Old Testament, Supplement series 320 (Sheffield: Sheffield Academic Press, 2000), 40–71.

tractive physical qualities, are not the basis of a relationship the young man should seek. The proverb instructs him to avoid at all costs lusting in his heart after such a woman. Behind the proverb, and entwined in its warning, is the understanding that physical attraction and passion are natural experiences for any young man. The clear warning attached is that this natural phenomenon can be the occasion of the downfall of any young man. Wisdom warns him that if he does not take heed, he will be reduced to a loaf of bread (v. 26).[6]

> Poverty is the object almost of horror to the greater part of men. The desire of removing or preventing it, is the grand spring which keeps the world constantly in motion. But the adulterer drives on furiously towards it, for though as much afraid of it as other men, he is hurried along in his wild career by tyrannizing passions, that have blinded his eyes, and taken possession of his soul to such a degree, that he must have them gratified, though ruin be the inevitable consequence.[7]

As the wise young reader follows the wisdom of the text before him, he recognizes and appreciates the astute counsel of his parents. He heeds their warnings, and purposes in his heart not to give up his life and his soul for an empty passion. The adulterous woman, though she hunts eagerly, will not find him receptive.

After all, he continues to read, one cannot play with fire without getting burned. He is confident that his parents and the proverb are right in steering him away from such a woman. He knows that he cannot walk on hot coals without burning his feet (vv. 27-28). If he wishes to be happy and prosperous, he must avoid this wicked woman at all costs, for she would lead him to ruin.

In the next picture the text paints, the young reader sees the man who would dare to go in to his neighbor's wife and have a physically and emotionally intimate relationship with her. He reads that a man is not despised if he steals bread because he is hungry. But if a man steals bread to satisfy his gluttony and greed, he will not go unpunished (vv. 29-31). In that circumstance no

---

[6] Here I am following the translation of this difficult Hebrew text as found in the New American Standard Bible.
[7] Lawson, *Proverbs*, 124.

repayment plan will be offered; no compensation for his misdeeds will be accepted.

The young man who fails to heed these warnings lacks sense (v. 32). The one who follows the course condemned here brings on his own punishment; he has no one to blame but himself, because he has been fairly warned. He can connect the truth of the proverb with the teachings and admonitions of his parents.

The son who reads these words is aware that if he fails to heed these warnings, disgrace and trouble will follow him. At the least, he will be an outcast and a hunted man. Having embarked on a course from which he cannot turn back, his life will be ruined by his own stupidity.

He will then have to face a jealous and enraged husband, and a community that will shun him. The young reader who is wise enough to heed his parents' warnings will read this proverb and see that there will be no mercy for him, should he be guilty of such a sin. Instead, the wrath of the estranged and wounded husband will be great and enduring.

Nothing the young man could do at this point would assuage the anger and vengeance of the violated husband (vv. 34-35). Fire would burn in the bosom of the wronged husband, and there would be no end to his judgment. And this retribution would be mild compared to the fact that the youth may lose his life at the hands of the jealous husband.

Though the young man might attempt to give many gifts, blood may be the only thing that would satisfy the husband. His parents' words ring loudly in his ears as he contemplates the truth of this series of proverbs. He will be a wise reader/responder if he heeds the warnings and disciplines of his parents. Should he exercise wisdom and adhere to what he has been taught, his days will be long and prosperous and free of guilt, shame, and fear.

The text will be validated. Either the young man will heed the warnings and have a peaceful and prosperous adult life, or his failure and misery will prove the scriptures true. His response will tell the tale.

As he returns to the opening of this passage, he recognizes that what his parents have faithfully attempted to instill in him are timeless and eternal truths. The text validates his parents' teaching, and it creates a blueprint for his life. By taking their warnings to heart, his life will be in line with the teachings of the law.

This young man's wise choice to heed the warnings will allow him to teach his own children the same truths, to pass on the text that has become a guidepost for him. The truth is timeless. Its validation comes through obedience or the lack thereof.

Today, as a young man reads this timeless passage, he too can avoid pitfalls before him. He too can find peace and prosperity amid a crooked and perverse generation. What was true for a modest young Hebrew boy long ago is still true today. As today's young reader opens his eyes and his mind to this passage, he will find its truth either through practicing it or through failing to do so.

The text seeks to warn and to teach. The reader/responder must seek it out and obey its principles. When he does so, life will be peaceful and joyful. Failure will result in a lifetime of misery and regret.

Chapter 3

Reclaiming the woman of substance
Proverbs 31:10–31

Jenifer Eriksen-Morales

One late afternoon a few years ago, I was waiting impatiently at a stoplight on my way to pick up my son at the babysitter's house. It had been a long and busy day at work, and I still needed to make a trip to the grocery store, have dinner, and attend a meeting at church. In that moment I realized that in an attempt to avoid being trapped by one lie, I had embraced another. Determined to prove that a woman's worth is not dependent on her home, husband, and children, I had adopted the lie that women can have it all and do everything superbly. In that brief pause in my frenzied life, I acknowledged that it is impossible for a woman to have, be, and do it all. I had been lied to by the media, my feminist role models, and even the Bible. Feeling betrayed and inadequate, I found myself quoting Proverbs 31 and asking sarcastically, "A capable wife, who can find?" One thing was certain, in that moment I realized I was not she, but I wanted to be, and for that reason I hated her.

I, like many women throughout generations, want to be the capable wife, mother, and worker described in Proverbs 31:10–31. I want to claim this woman as my model, as myself, but instead I loathe her, because try as I might, her perfection is impossible to achieve. Though no one knows for sure the identity of the woman described in this text, she serves as a model of the perfect woman. And she sets the standard high. Many Judeo-Christian women have been taught to hold the Proverbs 31 wife in high regard. Traditionally, Jewish husbands read this passage to their wives at the start of Shabbat. Christian books and Web sites offer suggestions

---

Jenifer Eriksen-Morales earned a Master of Divinity degree from Associated Mennonite Biblical Seminary in May 2007. She is minister of transitional ministries for Franconia Mennonite Conference. She is a member of Alpha Mennonite Church in Alpha, New Jersey. Jenifer and her husband, Victor Morales, have two children.

for becoming the Proverbs 31 woman. Drawn to her ideal, women study Proverbs 31, looking for ways to better themselves.

Lay people and biblical scholars interpret this passage in a variety of ways but with one consistency: the fear of the Lord is this woman's foundation (Prov. 31:30). Her mysterious identity and the foundation of her faith are her gift. As people struggle to identify with her and model themselves on her example, they discover her foundation in God. In order to claim her, they must claim her foundation. And when they do that, they let go of the need to mimic her slavishly.

While people claim to want to be like the woman described in Proverbs 31, her identity is unclear. Some consider her the personification of wisdom. Some believe she is one wife. Others think she is a composite of many. She has been used by those who argue that women's work is in the home, and by those who argue that women should work outside the home. By some she has been called independent; others see her as a doormat who gives herself for her household and for others.

This woman is elusive in part because of inconsistent translations of the Hebrew word *ḥayil*. This word in this context could describe a wife of strength, wealth, property, ability, diligence, wisdom, bravery, nobility, wisdom, virtue, or character. And the list continues. Many modern biblical translations name the Proverbs 31 woman a capable, virtuous, or noble wife. In an effort to gather together the many possible meanings of the word, I will follow Christine Roy Yoder in calling her a woman of substance.[1]

Although there are many definitions of the word *ḥayil*, its use in the Bible to describe women is rare. It appears only two other times, in Proverbs 12:4, and to describe Ruth (Ruth 3:11). In his essay "The Wife of Noble Character," Tom R. Hawkins asserts that Boaz acknowledged Ruth as "a woman of strength who knew how to achieve the object she pursued. She is a woman who purposefully, forcefully knew how to shape the circumstances to suit her needs."[2] Hawkins then translates comments by Hanneke van der Sluis and Douwe van der Sluis, who argue that evidence of the Proverbs 31

---
[1] See Christine Roy Yoder, "The Woman of Substance: A Socioeconomic Reading of Proverbs 31:10–31," *Journal of Biblical Literature* 122 (2003): 427–46.
[2] Tom R. Hawkins, "The Wife of Noble Character in Proverbs 31:10–31," *Bibliotheca Sacra* 153 (January–March 1996): 14.

woman's strength is found in verses 17 and 19-20, which "radiate strength and self assurance and indicate an almost aggressive approach to life."[3] According to these two authors, physical strength and strength of character are both evident in the poem. Clearly, strength of character and capability, along with the fear of the Lord, are important attributes of this woman.

But who is she? Because the description of the woman of substance follows words to King Lemuel from his mother, some interpreters believe the woman is the kind of wife the king's mother thinks he should find. Hawkins believes, however, that Proverbs 31:10-31 is not necessarily related to Proverbs 31:1-9, because there is no indication that Lemuel was seeking or commanded to seek such a wife, and the wife is not described as a queen or even a would-be queen. In fact, the woman of substance is married to a noble man or elder.[4]

Other scholars believe the woman of substance is a personification of wisdom. According to Hawkins, Michael Hermanson identifies the skillful woman found in Proverbs 1-9 with wisdom, and the unfaithful wife with folly. "These two figures in Proverbs 1-9 become 'representative examples of wisdom and folly through implied comparison.' In [Hermanson's] view 31:10-31 becomes the climactic *personification* of wisdom."[5] Thomas McCreesh agrees, because the woman of substance is described in terms similar to those used for Lady Wisdom in Proverbs 1-9.[6] But while there are many parallels between Lady Wisdom and the woman of substance, it seems doubtful that they are the same. Roy Zuch makes an excellent point: "Since the noble wife speaks with wisdom (v. 26), it makes no sense to equate Lady Wisdom with her and thus have 'Wisdom speaking with wisdom.'[7] It therefore seems better to see the Proverbs 31 noble woman as a 'wise woman, not wisdom personified.'"[8] This explanation does not satisfy all scholars. Albert Wolters thinks the woman of substance is both wisdom personified and a wise

---

[3] Ibid.
[4] Ibid., 13.
[5] Ibid., 15.
[6] Ibid., 17.
[7] For an in-depth description of the parallels between the Noble Wife and Lady Wisdom, see Hawkins, "The Wife of Noble Character."
[8] Ibid.,18.

woman. He writes, "The Song of the Valiant Woman is a portrait in verbs.... In a word, she is pictured as wisdom in action."[9]

So the debate continues: is she wisdom in action, a woman who acts wisely, or as some believe, just a typical woman? Hawkins claims she was a "woman doing what women do."[10] "What she is represented as doing is possible for an actual woman of the first millennium B.C. In this sense her existence is historically plausible."[11] But is it? The tasks this woman accomplishes are many and diverse. Just thinking about them makes me tired: she spins and sews, shops, manages servants, teaches her children, gardens, runs a business, and buys property—all the while keeping her husband and children happy.

More plausible is Christine Roy Yoder's view that the woman is a composite of Persian-period women, particularly women of affluence or position.[12] Her research on the social-historical world of Persian Palestine reveals that women of affluence fit the description in Proverbs 31:10–31. For example, such a woman would come to a marriage with a large dowry. She would be seen as a valuable bride, whose resources her husband would have at his disposal; hence the claim in verse 11b that her husband will never lack gain. In addition, in the Persian period, women of high rank were often property owners and had servants. Furthermore, Yoder's research shows that during this time, many women were workers who contributed to the larger economy. A woman of high status could well have been a supervisor or manager of workers.[13] Yoder writes, "The Woman of Substance is arguably a composite image of real women. She embodies not one woman, but rather the desired attributes of many."[14] Yoder continues, "Although based on real women, Proverbs 31:1–10 remains a portrait of the most desirable woman, an image of the ideal wife intended for a predominantly male audience."[15] In its context, the woman is praised but also objectified, bought with a dowry.

---

[9] Albert Wolters, "Proverbs XXXI 10-31 as Heroic Hymn: A Form Critical Analysis," *Vetus Testamentum* 37 (1988): 454.
[10] Hawkins, "The Wife of Noble Character," 18.
[11] Ibid., 16.
[12] Yoder, "The Woman of Substance," 429.
[13] Ibid., 436–45.
[14] Ibid., 446.
[15] Ibid.

Today, the Proverbs 31 woman continues to be objectified. She is known not for who she is but for what she does. Too often the woman of substance is a yardstick used to measure women's accomplishments; compared to her, whoever is being measured will come up short. It is no wonder that throughout history, women have at the same time sought to imitate her, competed with her, and held her in disdain. The objectification of women will continue as long as women allow themselves to be defined and measured according to works and achievements. In order to reclaim the woman of substance as a healthy role model, she must be given an identity based on who she is, not on owhat she does.

To do so, we need to read and study this passage in the spirit in which it was first written—as a celebration of relationship with Wisdom. Proverbs 31:10-31 is a poem. It is written as a perfect Hebrew acrostic. The author uses the passage to praise and celebrate a woman strong in character, stature, and intellect, who lives wisely. Wolters writes, "The acrostic poem glorifies the active good works of a woman in the ordinary affairs of family, community, and business life—good works for all their earthliness are rooted in the fear of the Lord. . . . The point of the song then becomes . . . not the praiseworthy ideal, but concrete practical wisdom rooted in the fear of the Lord."[16]

To reclaim the woman of substance, we must come to see wisdom as the fear of the Lord, and we must see her as a woman in relationship with God. Her actions stem from this relationship, and that relationship enables her to meet her full potential as woman, wife, mother, career woman. Because the woman of substance is the unified image of many strong and gifted women, readers are able to realize that this passage does indeed express truth about being a woman. Here it is. A woman is not capable of being all she expects or wants to be; she is not capable of being whatever another may expect or want her to be. Instead, a woman is capable of being and doing whatever she chooses to be. To be sure, the choices she makes may require sacrifice in another area of life. Realizing she is in control of the choices she makes, and not controlled by them, gives her power and confidence and sets her on the path of wisdom and empowerment. True freedom—to make choices that determine

---

[16] Wolters, "Proverbs XXXI 10-31," 457.

the direction of lives, equip herself and others for the future, and motivate herself and others to get through demanding everyday circumstances and overcome adversity—comes from relationship with God. It does not arise from perfect performance.

Because the woman of substance fears the Lord, she inspires women throughout history to reach their full potential. Her message speaks to many different people groups. The woman of substance "is a concrete word picture of all that it means to live wisely. . . . She does not follow the world's standards of feminine achievement. . . . Instead she has chosen to anchor herself on the 'fear of Yahweh.'"[17] She brings the message that when we are grounded in God's love, we can reach our full potential.

---

[17] Hawkins, "The Wife of Noble Character," 22.

Chapter 4

Who is this wisdom to whom we sing?
Job 28

Samuel Voth Schrag

After readers of the book of Job have traversed the tragic narrative introduction, and been buffeted about by the complex, repetitive, and angry debate between Job and his friends, they encounter a long soliloquy by Job, before Elihu gives his final word and God comes in the whirlwind. This soliloquy, chapters 27–31, reprises many of Job's previous themes. Innocent people suffer (and Job in particular suffers), and God is cruel, despite Job's virtue. In this speech, chapter 28 provides a dramatic contrast. The tone of this "hymn to wisdom" is strikingly different from that of all the text that comes before and after, and it does not fit easily within the narrative stream of Job. Yet it is hard to dismiss the text as a later addition. "Despite the clear delineations, Job 28 remains, as [Norman] Habel has observed, 'a brilliant but embarrassing poem for many commentators,'" because of the strong linguistic and thematic connections between this poem and Job as a whole.[1]

This odd but elegant text has many facets worth examining, but there are three exegetical questions that I find most pressing. First, what role (if any) does this text play in the larger narrative of Job? Second, what does the text have to say about wisdom in relationship to God and humanity? Third, what is the place of verse 28 in the structure both of chapter 28 and of Job as a whole? I have found no conclusive answers to these questions, but I will highlight the arguments I find most intriguing.

Samuel Voth Schrag is pastor of the Saint Louis Mennonite Fellowship. He is a 2007 graduate of Associated Mennonite Biblical Seminary, with a Master of Divinity degree. He graduated in 2004 from Bethel College in North Newton, Kansas. Samuel was born and raised in Wichita, Kansas, and is married to Rachel Voth Schrag.

[1] Samuel E. Balentine, *Job*, Smyth & Helwys Bible Commentary (Macon, GA: Smyth & Helwys Publishing, 2006), 415.

What role does Job 28 play in the larger narrative?

First, there is the broad question of whether the hymn to wisdom belongs in the larger narrative and, if it does belong, how it functions there. Most scholars agree that it is "an independent lyrical poem,"[2] in the sense that its function is not dependent on the larger text of Job. However, the precise level of its independence is debated. Scholars range from rejecting the poem as completely foreign and extraneous to the original Job narrative, to claiming it is "integral to the Book of Job,"[3] to a position somewhere in the middle. One scholar asserts, for example, that "the style of the chapter is both similar to and different from that of the Dialogue and of the God speeches. This is precisely the condition we would expect if it emanates from the same author in a different period of his career."[4]

I have already mentioned the most obvious reasons to see this poem as a separate entity: It falls awkwardly right in the middle of a passionate soliloquy from Job and does not seem to be either in Job's voice or in the voice of any of the other characters we have met thus far. Further, the poem has some unique vocabulary. "The Divine epithet [adonai] in v. 28 occurs nowhere else in the book; JHVH only in 12:9 in a quotation from Isaiah, [elohim] occurs only twice elsewhere in the book (5:8; 20:29), while the Divine names [el] and [shaddai], used over 90 times in the book, do not appear here at all."[5]

Despite these challenges, the hymn has significant linguistic ties to the rest of Job. First, although a bit of poetry seems somewhat out of place, a further explication of the meaning of wisdom fits well into Job's larger quest to understand his suffering. Reframing his quest as that of one who is seeking wisdom fits with the response he later receives from God. And it is not as if the reader should be surprised by odd changes in style in Job. Although the dialogue between Job and the three friends fits together as a consistent narrative whole, the final chapters of the book are more haphazard. Nor is it surprising to see complex and seemingly contradictory

---

[2] Robert Gordis, *The Book of Job: Commentary, New Translation and Special Studies* (New York: Jewish Theological Seminary of America, 1978), 298.
[3] Norman C. Habel, "Of Things Beyond Me: Wisdom in the Book of Job," *Currents in Theology and Mission* 10, no. 3 (June 1983): 144.
[4] Gordis, *The Book of Job*, 536.
[5] Ibid.

positions in Job. The entire book is set up dialogically, both in the discourse of Job and his friends and in the way the "prose narratives at the beginning and end of the book are set over against the poetic material in the middle."[6] Rather than being a later addition to Job, this poem may simply be one of several examples within the book of theological tension that goes unresolved.

In addition, there are parallels in the hymn to other sections of Job, including the narrative prologue, God's speech, and the dialogue with the three friends. The argument that wisdom is impossible to find harks back to Zophar's claim in 11:7–12,[7] and the vision of wisdom discovered in creation foreshadows God's arguments in chapters 38–41. Verse 28 explains that the fear of the Lord is wisdom, and to shun evil is understanding, which is precisely what Job did, according to Job 1:1. Job even uses the metaphor of mining in 3:21, when he curses God, and the description of God uncovering things hid in darkness in 12:22 parallels the miners' work of bringing things to light, in 28:11.[8] The thematic ties between this hymn to wisdom and the rest of the text of Job seem strong enough to at least warrant an analysis of the purposes this text serves in the book.

I'd like to focus on three implications for how this hymn functions in the book of Job as a whole. First, from a narrative perspective, it serves as a pause—or a *fermata*, as one commentator has put it. The high tension of the text is momentarily relieved, while the long and grueling path to God's response is drawn out a little longer.[9]

Second, the hymn speaks both to the impossibilities of Job's quest and to the possibilities of finding wisdom. The metaphor of mining connects both to Job's quest for answers and to God's quest for wisdom. There is a relatively obvious analogy between Job's questing after wisdom and the miners' quest after gold and precious jewels. The essence of the conflict in the text is Job's refusal to accept as a final answer either the platitudes of his friends or God's silence. Just as miners go to the ends of the earth to uncover what

---

[6] Carol A. Newsom, "The Book of Job," in *The New Interpreter's Bible*, vol. 4 (Nashville: Abingdon Press, 1996), 529.
[7] Balentine, *Job*, 416.
[8] Gerald J. Janzen, *Job*, Interpretation: A Bible Commentary for Teaching and Preaching (Atlanta: John Knox Press, 1985), 194.
[9] Balentine, *Job*, 417.

they covet, so Job turns every stone in a quest for an explanation for his suffering.

At the same time, the miners' work parallels God's. Like God (in 12:22), the miners bring light to what is in darkness (28:3). In verse 28:7, they search out the ends of the earth, where even the birds do not see, which is precisely how far God had to go when seeking wisdom (28:21).[10] And this double metaphor is not the only connection between Job's quest for wisdom and God's.

What does Job 28:28 say about wisdom in relation to God and humanity?

According to this hymn, wisdom is not innate in God; rather God discovered her in the process of ordering creation. "Wisdom is explicitly portrayed as a discrete entity with a 'place' of her own and a 'way' to that place."[11] Even "more surprising still is the idea that *God's capacity* to find wisdom by exercising it is in some way *human-like*. The four verbs in v. 27 . . . are generic. . . . These four verbs may be used with reference to both divine and human activity."[12] Although Job may be frustrated in his quest for understanding and wisdom, the subtext of this hymn to wisdom hints at parallels between human and divine realities. Wisdom may be totally inaccessible (v. 13); however, it may simply be hidden and almost entirely out of reach (v. 21).[13] This hymn is embedded in the narrative just when Job reaches his lowest point. He is at the end of his rope and is dwelling on his misery, and we have to slog through the torturous words of Elihu before we arrive at the end of the text. But this hymn holds out the promise of wisdom and insists that while it is unknowable, it exists; there is a foundational order to reality that grounds creation.[14] The question is how to get to it—and that question leads us to the conclusion of chapter 28.

What is the place of verse 28 in chapter 28 and in the book of Job?

It is impossible to analyze Job 28 without undertaking a closer examination of verse 28:

---

[10] Ibid., 422.
[11] Habel, "Of Things Beyond me," 144.
[12] Balentine, *Job*, 427.
[13] Ibid., 424.
[14] Habel, "Of Things Beyond Me," 145.

> And he said to humankind,
> "Truly, the fear of the Lord, that is wisdom;
>   and to depart from evil is understanding."

The verse is incongruous. Here at the end of a poem is a prose text with rhetorical ties to the prologue. This verse seems to suggest that humanity can gain wisdom, when the rest of the poem (and the rest of Job) insists that wisdom is out of human reach. And finally, it seems trite in comparison to the vast questing and unanswerable challenge of the rest of the book. But these facets of the text do not necessarily demand that the verse be excised, dismissed as a later addition, a vain attempt to render Job more orthodox.

This verse may be a straightforward conclusion to the poem. There is the divine wisdom, *hahokmah* (with a definite article), and there is human wisdom, *hokmah* (without a definite article). Humans cannot achieve divine wisdom (vv. 12 and 20), but they can fear God, shun evil, and achieve human wisdom.[15] This conclusion seems similar to Job's, when Job confesses to "things too wonderful for me" (42:3).

Next, the verse may invite the reader to redefine what it means to fear the Lord and shun evil. During Job's long fight with his friends, he does not seem to display the classic signs of fear of God. In fact, he is roundly rebuked for his insolence. Nevertheless, this poem reminds us that Job is described by the narrator—and by God—as a righteous man, and the epilogue confirms his status. If Job is righteous, then calling God to task for injustice must in some way fit together with fear of God.[16]

Finally, the verse may function ironically. In her commentary on Job, Carol Newsom puts forward a fascinating argument: "Perhaps the affront is part of the artistic design and pedagogical strategy. Readers are accustomed to finding the meaning of the work at the end . . . so here, even though the poem has been at pains to tell us that wisdom is not a thing to be located and extracted, we have still been expecting to find the extractable nugget at the end. To be met with dross instead of gold is disconcerting."[17]

I find this argument particularly interesting, because God's speech at the end of Job also functions in some ways as a trite (though more

---

[15] Gordis, *The Book of Job*, 539.
[16] Habel, "Of Things Beyond Me," 153.
[17] Newsom, "Job," 533.

dramatic) conclusion, rehashing old arguments from the friends and Elihu and failing to answer Job's questions.

In conclusion, chapter 28 seems to be a simple poem, but it plays a complicated role in the book of Job as a whole. It acts to foreshadow the voice of God and to reprise Job's quest for wisdom, but it also moves the drama forward by using a different style to explore what wisdom is and how humans can best relate to it.

Chapter 5

Job's legal defense
Job 31

Renee Kanagy

Job's speeches direct angry confusion toward God: Job feels forgotten, neglected, and unjustly punished. In chapter 31, he launches a final defense of his innocence. It takes the form of a list of transgressions he swears he has not committed. His mounting list resembles a plea for a legal trial.

Why does Job choose to communicate with God using oaths that evoke a trial setting? I believe that Job addresses God in legal metaphor because it is the strongest rhetorical tool his cultural setting offers. Based on what Job knows of God's nature and function through a covenantal relationship, Job understands that his appeal to God is justified and urgent.

Legal metaphor as effective rhetorical tool

Job labors to present his purity by using a series of self-clearance oaths.[1] In the course of outlining specific unrighteous behaviors and attitudes he swears he has not participated in, he demonstrates that he has not only fulfilled but exceeded the demands of the moral and ethical codes. The list of self-clearance oaths is a final attempt to assert his innocence in the face of afflictions he understands as punishment for sin. Job's innocence is the foundation of his identity as a righteous man.

This chapter is a last attempt on Job's part to call God to put the world back in order. When the righteous are punished, Job's faith convictions and his worldview begin to crumble. He uses

---

Renee Kanagy graduated from Associated Mennonite Biblical Seminary in May 2008 with a Master of Divinity degree, and she is pastor of New Creation Fellowship in Newton, Kansas. She and her husband Bradley Kauffman and their daughter live in Hesston, Kansas.

[1] Carol A. Newsom, *The Book of Job: A Contest of Moral Imaginations* (New York: Oxford University Press, 2003), 183.

strong language to make the case for his innocence and to plead for a reversal of the punishment. Susannah Ticciati's study of Job's ethical code in relationship to the law describes his motive for using legal terminology: "Job has no other option but to describe his integrity in legal terms; there is no other language available to him. He must do so, then, in such a way that the legal points beyond itself. It is for this reason, and not because Job is deluded or arrogant about his righteousness, that the resulting picture is one of inconceivable saintliness."[2] In what follows, we will explore the further meaning lying behind Job's communication to God through legal metaphor.

Job uses legal terminology throughout this chapter. The opening and closing remarks of his argument are couched in trial language. In the opening, he refers to the covenant with his eyes, the legal agreement between a master and servants, as the reason why he would not commit the list of unrighteous behaviors and attitudes. The closing remarks indicate that a legal indictment from God listing his sins would resolve Job's unjust punishment.

Scholars debate about the literary form or genre that Job fits into. Katherine Dell suggests that literary forms are intentionally misused throughout Job—as in the case of the negative oath used to assert innocence and request an audience with God. "Traditional forms from legal, cultic, and wisdom spheres are deliberately misused by the author to convey scepticism."[3] In her chapter examining form, she draws the conclusion that by intentionally misusing a variety of mini-forms, an overarching form of parody arises. This is true of the literary form of chapter 31 as well.

Example one of misuse of legal forms: Job swears his innocence in the form of several negative oaths in the body of the chapter.[4] While negative oaths were common in ancient Near Eastern writings, they were generally used to request mercy or forgiveness.

---

[2] Susannah Ticciati, *Job and the Disruption of Identity* (New York: T & T Clark International, 2005), 150.
[3] Katherine J. Dell, *The Book of Job as Sceptical Literature* (New York: Walter de Gruyter, 1991), 110.
[4] Scholars debate about the number of oaths present in the text. That debate is not central to my argument and is not included here.

Here, Job uses the form to persuade God to right the injustice of punishment falling on the innocent.[5]

Example two of misuse of legal forms: Job's goal to establish his purity is evident in the pattern of the stanzas. An unjust behavior is named and then paired with severe consequences which God has a role in executing. A survey cited by Dell of oaths in scripture reveals that consequences, or curses, are commonly left unwritten, for fear that stating the curse would bring it into being. The survey found only two complete oaths—ones containing consequences—outside the book of Job. In contrast, four complete oaths are included in Job.[6] Dell observes that "in saying things which are customarily left unsaid or at most concealed in the evasive oath-formula, the author of Job created a dramatic effect and asserted once and for all Job's innocence."[7] Using the oath in an unusual way serves to highlight Job's purity.

What does it means that this chapter both relies on legal form and deliberately misuses legal forms? Parody seems a stretch in this chapter of Job, but the misuse of form does have great persuasive appeal. Is it possible that the misuses of multiple forms point to a misuse of metaphor in expecting God to function only in specific ways?

How Job believes God acts

What motivates Job to use the form of legal oaths to appeal to God so vehemently and with such conflict? Framing his argument for his innocence as a plea for formal legal charges places the question of guilt on Job, not God. Carol Newsom suggests that this use of rhetoric allows Job to refrain from naming God as guilty while creating an opening for God to reverse judgment.[8] Job offers a win/win situation. His argument is formed in a way that parallels other scriptural texts in which a less powerful figure makes a case to more powerful authorities, as in the case of Judah and Tamar.[9]

---

[5] Samuel E. Balentine, *Job*, Smith & Helwys Bible Commentary (Macon, GA: Smyth & Helwys Publishing, 2006), 487.
[6] The curses are: vv. 8, 20, 22, 40. See Dell, *The Book of Job as Sceptical Literature*, 134.
[7] Ibid.
[8] Newsom, *Book of Job*, 197.
[9] Balentine, *Job*, 496.

The result of the argument is that the authority figure concedes, honorably dropping the erroneous charges.

Job hopes that after hearing his case, God will concede that Job is innocent. His approach seems to assume that God is actively involved in the world but somehow uninformed. Additionally, it assumes a kind of peer relationship with God. God can be called to accountability in the same way that powerful people can be. In a way, Job assumes that God is required to act as God calls people to act.

Job holding fast to his deuteronomic worldview

The second area of expectation is grounded in who Job understands God to be. Job expects God to manage the created world within the same system and rules God had established in covenanting with humanity. The end of the opening statement from Job states his belief in deuteronomic theology: "Surely calamity waits for the unrighteous and disaster for the workers of iniquity."[10] Job assumes that God rewards those who keep the law and punishes those who do not.

This working assumption seems to place control in God's hands; God rewards and punishes. But as Lyn Bechtel observes about deuteronomic theology in general,

> In actuality it is humans who are in control. In the dualistic world imagined by deuteronomic theology, people can choose between absolute righteousness and absolute wickedness. If they choose righteousness, God must reward them with life and prosperity. But if they choose wickedness, God must punish them with adversity and deprivation. Control is in the hands of the people who do the choosing, and God's function is reduced to adhering to a formula that satisfied the human ego.[11]

Job has no conception of God working outside this theological framework. As more and more of his experience conflicts with this

---

[10] Translation follows that by Robert Gordis, *The Book of Job: Commentary, New Translation, and Special Studies* (New York: Jewish Theological Seminary of America, 1978), 340.

[11] Lyn M. Bechtel, "A Feminist Approach to the Book of Job," in *A Feminist Companion to Wisdom Literature*, ed. Athalya Brenner (Sheffield: Sheffield Academic Press, 1995), 231.

theology, his appeal to God becomes more and more urgent—with this chapter as its most intense expression.

In the course of swearing several oaths, Job names acts of unrighteousness for which he says he would have deserved punishment, had he committed them. But most of what he names are not acts that could be prosecuted in court; they are violations of moral or ethical standards.[12] The list includes coveting women (v. 1), lying and deceiving (v. 6), adultery (v. 8), abusive use of power (v. 13), oppression of disenfranchised peoples (vv. 16–21), idolatrous trust in wealth and other gods (vv. 24, 27), seeking vengeance (vv. 29–31), refusing to extend hospitality (v. 32), and abuse of creation (v. 38).

When metaphors try to encompass God

Job had lived a life founded on covenantal relationship with God. His code of ethical and moral behavior surpasses any other list in scripture—including the New Testament.[13] Beyond that, Job is described in the book's prologue as a non-Israelite, dwelling in the land of Uz—somewhere in the East. Therefore, Job is not bound by the covenant but has chosen to place himself within it.[14] Yet in his exemplary faithfulness, Job fails to realize that using only the metaphor of the covenant limits his ability to know how God functions and who God is. "Job's image of God is developed out of the highest and best values of his society, values that Job has always tried to embody."[15]

This is a tension within which all who seek to know and follow God live: the tension between our intimate knowledge of God provided by our experience, and the unknowable nature of God. God is both "wholly other"[16] and revealed in particular social contexts. Job 31 is a vivid demonstration of Job's struggle to contain God within the boundaries of one set of metaphors. It reveals what happens when a metaphor comes to be understood as directly corresponding to the subject it describes, instead of illuminating an aspect of that subject.

---

[12] Balentine, *Job*, 475.
[13] Ibid., 471.
[14] Ibid., 493.
[15] Carol A. Newsom, "The Book of Job," in *The New Interpreter's Bible*, vol. 4 (Nashville: Abingdon Press, 1996), 556.
[16] Ibid.

Summary

Job expects God to respond to injustice with punishment and to justice with rewards, as God has called God's people to do. Job believes that God's character corresponds with the character of righteous people. These convictions arise from Job's sense that the metaphors of faith reveal and reflect not just part of who God but describe and define all that God is. In the face of evidence suggesting that this view of God is inadequate, Job persists in adhering to it. He uses the strongest language he has access to, even strengthening it by altering the use of legal forms, in his effort to demand that God restore order to Job's religious and social world. The energy and drive with which Job pursues a reordering of his life and world reveals the tenacity with which we can cling—even in the face of insurmountable evidence to the contrary—to our belief that our metaphors can hold the entire nature of God.

Chapter 6

Laying the foundations
God's appearance in Job 38–39

Tommy Boutell

Among God's qualities is a willingness to afflict the comfortable. Many years ago, as a pre-seminary student in my early twenties, God decided that the book of Job, and especially God's response to Job in chapters 38 and 39, would have a significant role in disturbing my spiritual comfort. Instead of keeping my eyes on Christ and on the call that I'd received, I obsessed about the hypocrisy of church leaders and incomprehensible misperceptions of who God is. These two chapters were my ticket out. They were my theological justification not only to leave the pre-seminary but also to trade in my Christian faith for a spiritual cafeteria tray piled with secular humanism and intellectualism.

I viewed God's initial response to Job in these two chapters as arrogant, nonresponsive, and bullying. I repeated the popular phrase, "*That's* not the type of God *I* want to worship." My context was the context of Job. My questioning didn't subside; it took on differing narratives. My self-dialogue was that of Bildad, Zophar, and Eliphaz. I needed answers, and I welcomed all Elihus who came to call. I remained in my humanistic orthodoxy for more than fifteen years. Providentially, my reconversion experience would reenter via Job 38 and 39. It followed the journey of Job both in the context of God's words and in the nature of my response to God's method of communication.

Contextually, God's speech in chapters 38 and 39 is a pre-climax to Job's response beginning in chapter 40:3–5, and continuing in 42:1. God appears when Job is at his most desperate, to exert power

---

Tommy Boutell is a Master of Divinity student at Associated Mennonite Biblical Seminary. He is pastor of Olivet United Methodist Church, Grand Rapids, Michigan, an inner city church meeting daily spiritual and material needs of people who are marginalized, homeless, and dealing with mental health and addiction recovery issues. He and Shelly, his wife, have three children.

through speech that is deliberately intended to avoid directly addressing Job's complaints. By setting this stage for Job's response, God speaks volumes. According to David Penchansky, God's speech in chapters 38 and 39 is not a commentary on either the righteousness or the blasphemy of Job.[1] I agree with this assessment. I would add that God's speech here is intended to force Job—and us as readers—to react to the absence of a clearly expressed divine resolution. God answers all Job's questions, but not in the way anyone expects. God's response comes in requiring Job to create his own God-image and his own interpretation of God's intentions, without direct resolution or assurance. How true to form the God of Job is; this God's modus operandi contrasts with that of the god so many of us experience today.

Job claims that he is devastated but faithful (1:20). He is in unimaginable agony (chapter 3), and he desperately wants his friends to see that he is the same old Job (6:24–30). He more than ever understands the futility of arguing with God (9:2). His friends have unjustly convicted him (chapter 10), and they proceed to add insult to injury. Job's ultimate argument is that he lacks a listening witness (19:23–29; chapter 21). Elihu, who—ironically—arrives as the advocate for Job, is supposed to answer all the questions the group has posed, to do so with clarity, and perhaps even to bring healing. Instead his words have the opposite effect. His statement that "God thunders and we cannot ignore" (37:5) amounts to criticism and condemnation of Job, dehumanizing him and his suffering.

It is in this bleak and almost morose moment that Job gets his audience with God. The "whirlwind of Sinai,"[2] as John Wesley referred to God's presence, appears and asks who it is that speaks about things he doesn't know. God's question is directed at Job but clearly also addresses Job's friends and generations to come. God begins, appropriately, by recapturing the spirit of his magnificence within Genesis, questioning Job about the creation of the heavens, the earth, the sea, and the origins of day and night (38:4–15). God then breaks from the Genesis outline, not touting the grandeur of the animals, humans, or the Sabbath; God instead refers to the

---

[1] David Penchansky, *The Betrayal of God: Ideological Conflict in Job* (Louisville: Westminster John Knox Press, 1990), 42–56.
[2] John Wesley, *Commentaries on Job,* Chapter 38; http://www.christnotes.org/commentary.php?com=wes&b=18&c=38.

majesty of his inanimate creations. God shakes the foundation of Job's orthodoxy. Job's conceptions of human "godliness," or at least of his uprightness and his certainty about God's natural order, are demolished. God shatters these accepted conventions by describing the depths and expanses of earth, divine control of death, light and darkness, space, and floods (38:16–38). Here God's focus on his own creative achievements keeps humanity out of the limelight.

God then talks about the living things in the natural world. God challenges Job to match the divine creativity evident in the grandeur and the comedy of God's creatures (38:39–39:30). The nourishment of lions and ravens, the birthing of goats and deer, and the freedom of the wild ox all show that God has placed things as he wishes them to be. God even points to the stupidity of the ostrich or the battling horse, which may have their raison d'être in God's idiosyncrasies or desire for amusement. Finally God points to the elements of created gracefulness in the hawk in flight and the nesting eagle.

God does not seem content, however, to allow "open interpretation"[3] or "asymmetric faith"[4] to suffice as his summation. Omnipotent division goes out the window as we move to the epilogue of Job. The magnitude of God spoken of in Job 38 and 39 seems to be negated, or at least humanized, by the contradictory simplicity of God's action in restoring Job. If the lesson we are supposed to learn is that we must worship God in spite of and because of God's great mystery, why would God cop out by throwing what amounts to a birthday party as a means of restitution? The epilogue of Job seems to be an ending based more on human desire than on maintaining the consistency of the story. God's answer is simply that there is no final answer, except that God is God.

This question of God's consistent nature, the influences from ancient Near Eastern literature, and arguments about the dating of the book of Job support the theological claim that God leaves us to wonder.[5] We wonder as we answer God in our own idioms. Job answered God in his own way, in eloquent simplicity: "Therefore

---

[3] Open interpretation is any interpretation of God that puts human needs over the will of God.
[4] In asymmetric faith, human interpretation is projected one way onto God, without God's revelation shaping what we believe.
[5] Penchansky, *The Betrayal of God*, 61, 87–91.

I have uttered what I did not understand, things too wonderful for me, which I did not know" (42:3). Adam Clarke's commentary paraphrases and interprets: "I acknowledge my ignorance; I confess my foolishness and presumption; I am ashamed of my conduct; I lament my imperfections; I implore thy mercy and beg thee to show me thy will, that I may ever think, speak, and do, what is pleasing in thy sight."[6]

Many modern interpretations of Job reach for easy answers or make connections that seem intended to comfort. Some conclude that Elihu is actually Jesus, or that the key to understanding Job is in valuing the quiet submission God requires: "God thus confirms Elihu's sentiment, that submission to, not reasonings on, God's ways is man's part. This and the disciplinary design of trial to the godly is the great lesson of this book."[7]

Job's answer, however, and the great lesson of the book, seems to be not as much about submission or even the disciplinary design of trial to the godly. Rather, it is informed by the human observation of the unknown nature of God. We can and should love the God we do not understand. We should also encourage others to be joyful about a God who allows or even causes calamity. Why? Well, there we go again: this approach is circular, paradoxical, and yet a wonderful part of our faith and God's message.

God is reaching out to us in love in chapters 38 and 39 of Job. God does not reach out to us in a way we can fully grasp, but there is substance there. God's vivid poetic descriptions of his accomplishments show us that he exists, that he has order, and that he is creatively in control. A close equivalent to this type of assurance is found in Psalm 99:1, 6-9:

> [1]The LORD is king; let the peoples tremble!
>   He sits enthroned upon the cherubim;
>   let the earth quake!
> [6]Moses and Aaron were among his priests,
>   Samuel also was among those who called on his name.
>   They cried to the LORD, and he answered them.

---

[6] *Adam Clarke's Commentary on the Bible* (Grand Rapids: Baker Book House, 1967); http://www.studylight.org/com/acc/view.cgi?book=job&chapter=042.
[7] Jamieson, Fausset and Brown's *Commentary on the Whole Bible* (Grand Rapids: Zondervan, 1961), Job 38:1; http://jfb.biblecommenter.com/job/38.htm.

> ⁷He spoke to them in the pillar of cloud;
>   they kept his decrees,
>   and the statutes that he gave them.
> ⁸O Lord our God, you answered them;
>   you were a forgiving God to them,
>   but an avenger of their wrongdoings.
> ⁹Extol the Lord our God,
>   and worship at his holy mountain;
>   for the Lord our God is holy.

I will read these chapters of Job throughout my life. Experience and referential exegesis[8] will affect my interpretation. I am open to the possibility that my understanding of Job could change again as radically as it has shifted over the past twenty years. My faith journey continues to include blessings and trials, and at least in part through my interpretation of these chapters, I will continue to define what it means for me to be a person of God. If there is a constant in my growth, it is the conviction that in Christ I have a sufficient intermediary to Job's God. I am committed to not giving up on the complexities of the answers in the book of Job, but I trust that through graceful faith, my grasping at God's answers or expectations can be less desperate. God's wisdom whirlwind cannot be separated from my worship or my larger God-image. The director of the Joban play will most certainly continue to reshape our pilgrimages. When the time is right, God will keep shaking things up. That will doubtless continue to be the case with Job's message for me.

---

[8] In referential exegesis, the hermeneutic comes from a rereading of scripture after more life experiences occur.

Chapter 7

Animals and humanity in the world
Job 38–39

Brianne Donaldson

Job 38–39 offers a picture of a creation-centered universe in which humanity and creatures are in dialectical relationship. It reveals kenosis, or self-limitation, as the grain of an aesthetic universe, which all creation is persuaded to mimic.

Creation-centered universe

Without question, the first Yahweh speech offers a unique glimpse of a powerful God symbolically defined against other deities of ancient Near Eastern mythology (38:8, 32, 38). The "war of words"[1] between Job and Yahweh introduces the four inexplicable spheres of earth, sea, heaven, and underworld,[2] and with them the artistry of a divine midwife who brought it all into being. Yahweh is a master architect, laying the earth's foundations and garnering the praise of the stars and the heavenly councils. The Lord is also a divine parent who wraps the newborn creation in swaddling clothes (38:9). Leo Perdue writes, "It is infant chaos, not human mortals, whom Yahweh nurtures."[3] Binding the creation in this way keeps chaos under control. Even light, which changes reality as it illuminates the shape of all things, cannot be contained by humans. In a corrective translation by Robert Gordis, Yahweh asks Job, "Can you

---

In May 2007 Brianne Donaldson earned a Master of Arts in theological studies, with an emphasis in theology and ethics, from Associated Mennonite Biblical Seminary. She currently lives in southern California, where she works as regional educational coordinator for the animal advocacy organization Vegan Outreach. She is pursuing a PhD in philosophy of religion at Claremont Graduate University, with an emphasis on human/animal nonviolence.

[1] Leo Perdue, *Wisdom and Creation: The Theology of Wisdom Literature* (Nashville: Abingdon Press, 1994), 169.
[2] Ibid., 170.
[3] Ibid., 171.

take light to its border? Can you trace its path home?" (38:19).[4] Light is shed on wickedness but also on those who defy the rule of God. The mysteries of death are preserved even further below the abyss of the sea, another phenomenon incomprehensible to human knowing.[5]

Additionally, the relationship between the Creator and the land and creatures is independent of humans.[6] In fact, human existence is unnecessary for the animals and natural phenomena seen in this text as under the intimate care of God.[7] The trust between the Creator and her creation is implicit in divine provision of what each animal needs for survival, "from instinct to food to the capacity to reproduce."[8] There is a movement from rebuking Job to instructing him in wonder. Yahweh puts Job in his place by stating what Job doesn't know, but at the same time God *proclaims* what Job doesn't know and points to "a world full of an emotional hum not assumed by Job's rationally grounded questioning of the deity."[9] Except the horse, the animals paired in these verses dwell in regions uninhabited by humans. These creatures do not fear or dread humanity (compare Gen. 9:2: "The fear and dread of you shall rest on every animal of the earth. . . ."). According to Perdue, many of the animals cited would have been "hunted by Ancient Near East kings in ritual acts designed to secure order in society and the cosmos." He continues: "In a striking repudiation of an anthropology in which humans are kings in God's creation, Yahweh speaks of sustaining a world hostile to human life. The anthropological tradition grounded in the metaphor of humanity as king is shattered. Dwelling in a reality that is not anthropocentric, Job receives no divine commission to go forth and subdue the cosmos."[10] The ethical workings of the universe are grounded in a

---

[4] Robert Gordis, *The Book of Job: Commentary, New Translation and Special Studies* (New York: Jewish Theological Seminary of America, 1978), 446–48.
[5] Perdue, *Wisdom and Creation,* 171; Gordis, *The Book of Job,* 445.
[6] Terence Fretheim, "The Earth Story in Jeremiah 12," in *Readings from the Perspective of the Earth,* ed. Norman Habel (Sheffield: Sheffield Academic Press, 2000), 99.
[7] Milton Horne, "From Ethics to Aesthetics: The Animals in Job 38:39–39:30," *Review and Expositor* 102 (Winter 2005): 133.
[8] Perdue, *Wisdom and Creation,* 174.
[9] Horne, "From Ethics to Aesthetics," 130.
[10] Perdue, *Wisdom and Creation,* 174.

kind of ordered rationality, but they also rest firmly on Yahweh's aesthetic appreciation of the universe for what it is.[11]

A dialectic of humanity and creatures

The distinction between the beautiful and the irrational is worth expanding. According to Horne, "the dialectic of anthropology and cosmology represents the best approach to expressing the theology of wisdom literature."[12] Job is not at creation's center. Placing the beautiful over against rational human justice is the means by which the Yahweh speeches teach Job about the ethical order of the universe. Set against the symbolic use of animals elsewhere in the book as signs of wealth and power (1:3), or as victims of religious sacrifice (1:5; 42:8), the animals in chapters 38–39 are not "mere possessions manipulated by human owners."[13] Neither are they used allegorically (as elsewhere in the book) to illustrate wicked (24:5; 30:29) or exemplary behavior (9:26). The images of 38–39 also take us in a direction different from that of the didactic concern about the relationship between humankind and God found earlier, in Elihu's contention that the Maker crafts humans wiser than the birds (35:11), for example.

The dialectic of 38–39 demonstrates that animals have value aside from human aims. Further, they have real lives given them by their Designer. The freedom of the wild donkey in 39:5 is indicated by its obstinacy and speed and general avoidance of humans. Writes Gordis, "The poet here adopts the limited perspective of man, who normally expects these animals to be in bondage for his benefit."[14] Fetters of humanity are not the ultimate authority for these animals. Gordis provides a more accurate translation of 39:1, "Do you know when the mountain goats give birth?," changing it to "Do you know about the lusts of the mountain goats?" The desires of animals can be seen, at least in part, as intentional and inspirational. Even the "unnatural behavior" of an ostrich who does not care for its young (39:13-18) is the handiwork of God, revealing the diverse character of creation, if one at variance from a rational model. The portrayal of the hawk or vulture (of 39:26, 30), with its

---
[11] Horne, "From Ethics to Aesthetics," 135.
[12] Ibid., 127.
[13] Ibid., 128.
[14] Gordis, *The Book of Job*, 456.

unique lifestyle needs, further upsets the human hierarchy. The bird God exults in, Gordis writes, "is not merely of no use to man, but actually feeds on his body."[15]

The parabolic use of animals requires that the teacher identify some similarities between humans and other animals, so the latter work as teaching models. But these chapters do not assign anthropomorphic qualities to animals; they do not accentuate traits that would make the animals seem human. Rather, these animals possess real cries, longings (38:41, 39:1), and even a laughter all their own (ox and ostrich); they serve as pedagogical instruments for Job's learning.

Self-limitation and the preservation of freedom

The ethical order of the universe comes through in lessons of beauty, divine provision, and intimate relation with "irrational" creatures in their own right. Humans are not the mediators of value to the universe. Animals and nature teach their own lessons to Job. Prominent among these lessons is a divine ontology radically different from the one evident in the traditional view of Job's friends. Although the swaddling control of the universe is intact, that control takes on a limited shape. The divine parameters of creation are not set through all-powerful coercion but through the preservation within creation of freedom to respond. The strange habits of the ostrich (39:17), the obstinacy of the wild donkey (39:7)—these behaviors are allowed. Just as the offspring of the deer "grow up in the open; go forth, and do not return to them" (39:4), neither does the ox return to any human crib (39:9). A divine acceptance allows things to be what they are. The wild ox has to give its "consent" (39:11), just as Job is free to serve and fear Yahweh gratuitously. Both are also free not to do so.[16]

The preservation of freedom requires a self-limiting God who is nothing like the retributive deity described by Eliphaz (4:9–11), "a destructive tyrant who overpowers and even brings to their end animals who do not yield to the divine will."[17] The whelps of the lioness are no longer scattered as in 4:11. Instead their particular longings are satisfied (38:39-40). Nature becomes a canvas on which

---

[15] Ibid., 463.
[16] Horne, "From Ethics to Aesthetics," 139.
[17] Ibid., 138.

the character of the universe is painted; we can participate in that change. A kenotic Creator preserves the freedom of creation's response by invitation and persuasion. Inevitably, this freedom will lead to some suffering and competition, but the kenotic God will not coerce things into being what they are not, by stealing their freedom and forcing compliance.

This kenotic disposition is represented in a pacifist example. By choosing not to kill an armed intruder, human kenosis or self-limitation may lead to suffering and perhaps the injury of others whom one's violence could protect. However, self-limitation, whether creaturely or divine, will not violate the grain of the universe. Mutual relationship and interdependence is the *imago Dei* that all creation is capable of imitating. Job 38–39 presents a cruciform theology that illumines the path humans should take to find their rightful relationship to the elements and particular creatures whose lives are affected by our actions: Let them be. Invite and persuade. Never coerce or subdue. Yahweh's aesthetic appreciation of a beautifully free universe, however irrational it may seem, grounds all ethical inquiry.

Closing

Job's appeal to human justice is corrected in these chapters. The divine speeches show that a formula of deeds and consequences is not adequate to "cover the complexity brought on by the needs for survival, of real freedom and choice or relationships between caregivers and care receivers, of simultaneous foolishness and beauty."[18] The invitation is to think theologically about the creation-centered world of Job, the true dialectic between the uniquely gifted lives of animals and the value imposed on them by humans. Readers of Job 38–39 witness a self-limiting Maker who shows humanity how to recover a sense of belonging among earth's creatures, and a challenge to reconsider our relationship with nonhuman animals within our daily actions and within systems of consumption.

---

[18] Ibid., 140.

Flinging ourselves upon the impossible
Job 38-39 and human suffering through the eyes of liberation theology

Elizabeth Miller

The story of Job is a story of individual suffering, but the questions Job asks are universal. In *On Job: God-Talk and the Suffering of the Innocent*, Gustavo Gutiérrez, a native of Peru and a prominent Latin American liberation theologian, extends the context of Job to that of the people of Ayacucho, Peru, "who, like Job, suffer unjustly and cry out to the God of life."[1] Throughout the 1980s and early 1990s, conflict between the Maoist guerrilla group Sendero Luminoso (SL) and the Peruvian military transformed the highland province of Ayacucho in Peru into a place of terror. Children were taken to be soldiers for SL, while thousands of people simply disappeared. Communities faced the impossible demand that they declare loyalty to both SL and the army. If the guerrillas suspected a village of disloyalty, they would force its residents into the town square and slit their throats.

In 1990, U.S. ambassador to Peru Anthony Quainton sent a confidential state department cable observing that "one cannot appear neutral in Ayacucho and survive. If you are radical right, only SL tries to kill you. If you are a terrorist, only the police and military try to kill you. If you are in the middle, both the terrorists and the soldiers want you dead."[2] In response to this situation,

---

Elizabeth Miller is a theological studies student at Associated Mennonite Biblical Seminary. She lives in Goshen, Indiana, and attends Berkey Avenue Mennonite Fellowship. Elizabeth is a member of Hopedale Mennonite Church in Illinois.

[1] Gustavo Gutiérrez, *On Job: God-Talk and the Suffering of the Innocent* (Maryknoll, NY: Orbis Books, 1985), dedication page.
[2] "Peru 'In the Eye of the Storm': Declassified U.S. Documentation on Human Rights Abuses and Political Violence," The National Security Archive Electronic Briefing Book No. 64, ed. Tamara Feinstein, 22 January 2002; http://www.gwu.edu/~nsarchiv/NSAEBB/NSAEBB64/.

whole villages left Ayacucho, abandoning the Andes, so central to Quechua identity, for the dry sand-dune slums of Lima. As a result of death and displacement, population in the province declined by 3.5 percent overall and 23 percent in rural areas, even as the nation's population increased.[3] The story of Sendero Luminoso in Peru is a story of the great suffering of thousands of individuals, of hundreds of communities, and of a nation. "How are we to do theology while Ayacucho lasts?" asks Gutiérrez. "How are we to speak of the God of life when cruel murder on a massive scale goes on in 'the corner of the dead'?"[4]

Although his context of suffering is different, Job also questions the ways his community speaks of God. Ultimately, he challenges God's justice, because Job sees not only himself but many other innocents, among whom those from Ayacucho may be included, suffering unjustly. The Yahweh speeches in Job 38–40 address Job's questions about justice by expounding the plan and design (*'etsah*) of God. Through these speeches, God is freed from human conceptions of justice, even as humanity is freed to demand and practice justice in light of God's design. Gutiérrez argues that it is possible for us to accept such an unbounded God, because God's divine justice is expressed in a unique context of gratuitous love.

As we become aware of the suffering of others, Job's experience becomes ours. We recognize the love given in God's *'etsah*, which frees God from our conceptions of justice and allows us to participate in the unfolding of justice. Although Job's suffering is originally understood as an isolated, individual experience, Job slowly broadens his perspective "to include the sufferings and injustices to which the poor fall victim."[5] In Job 24, the suffering of victims and the trespasses of oppressors are exposed. The poor in ancient Israel were those who were left without any defenses, guardians, or property. Without such safeguards, they were pushed to the hidden margins of society.[6] Job's recognition of these innocent others forces him to reject with finality the doctrine of retribution his

---

[3] "Facts: Ayacucho in Peru," *New Internationalist* (March 2000); http://findarticles.com/p/articles/mi_m0JQP/is_321/ai_30301540.
[4] Gutiérrez, *On Job*, 102.
[5] Ibid., 37.
[6] Norman C. Habel, *The Book of Job* (Philadelphia: Westminster Press, 1985), 359.

friends espouse.⁷ With this understanding, however, Job's demand for justice only increases.

In the speeches of Yahweh, a vision of divine justice (*mishpat*) unfolds. Both aspects of divine justice discussed in chapters 38–40 illuminate *'etsah* as a central theme. It is clear that wisdom and order may be found in *'etsah*, God's plan and design. Yahweh explains that the sea is hedged, both darkness and light have their proper ways, the constellations form according to celestial laws, and wisdom governs the clouds of heaven.⁸ All this explanation serves to reveal the depth of God's design and its unfathomable nature. Instead of the retributive God-human relationship argued by Job's friends, in which God repays righteousness with material blessing just as readily as God punishes unrighteousness, Gutiérrez sees gratuitous love in Yahweh's revelation. Such love is especially evident in 38:12–15, 25–27.⁹

One of Job's accusations against God has been that the wicked enjoy prosperity even while the innocent suffer. How can justice be present in such a context? In 38:12–15, Yahweh describes the action of the dawn. The *'etsah* of God has assigned dawn its place as regulator of the rhythm of night and day and as that which "controls the operations of the wicked."¹⁰ Yahweh speaks:

> ¹²Have you ever in your life given orders to the morning
>   or sent the dawn to its post,
> ¹³to grasp the earth by its edges
>   and shake the wicked out of it?
> ¹⁴She turns it red as a clay seal,
>   she tints it as though it were a dress,
> ¹⁵stealing the light from evildoers
>   and breaking the arm raised to strike.¹¹

Gutiérrez interprets the balance between night and dawn as an expression of the gratuitousness of God's love, expressed in the very balance of the universe. Dawn, as a part of Yahweh's *'etsah*, plays an active role in the unfolding of justice. The problem of innocent suffering is not answered, but God's design shows a balance,

---

⁷ Gutiérrez, *On Job*, 47.
⁸ Habel, *The Book of Job*, 530–31.
⁹ Gutiérrez, *On Job*, 72.
¹⁰ Habel, *The Book of Job*, 540.
¹¹ Gutiérrez, *On Job*, 71; citing Job 38:12–15 (New Jerusalem Bible).

evidenced here by the counterparts of light and darkness. Even while the wicked operate in the darkness, "with each dawn they are exposed and contained."[12] The prosperity of the wicked does not progress indefinitely. Even if the dawn does not necessarily result in the destruction of the wicked, exposure of injustice is lovingly built into *'etsah*.[13]

In verses 25–27, Yahweh explains the presence of *'etsah*, even in the unseen places of earth. Grass grows and rain falls in those places no human has ever inhabited. God's design for fresh grass in the corners of the earth is a "mark of unsolicited goodness" and gratuitous love.[14] From the perspective of Job and the communities of Ayacucho, God's love is reassuring, yet it still does not directly answer the questions of justice.

For Gutiérrez, these passages also demonstrate God's respect for human freedom. Justice is not dictatorially imposed on humanity. Rather it is processive, unfolding in the rhythm of night to day, expanding under rainstorms in the most remote desert canyons. This also is a sign of mercy and love, reminding us that just as the wicked may not always be wicked, so the righteous may not always be righteous.[15] Just as a processive justice glorifies God's mercy and love, it also highlights the degree to which God respects human freedom—enough to enact justice as a process, not as a singular act.[16]

Despite the respect with which God treats human freedom, Job 38–39 presents humanity as only one small part of God's *'etsah*. Given its position, humanity must not apply its conditions for justice to God. Yahweh recounts the creation of the animal world in chapter 39, focusing on the wonders of each creature. Yahweh oversees the freedom of the wild ass, gives strength to the horse, and imparts wisdom to the wings of the hawk. Even in its rejection of an anthropocentric worldview, this chapter points to Yahweh's care and providence for wild animals, in order to reassure humanity of Yahweh's concern for human life. This care and providence are implicitly extended to Job and to those in Ayacucho.[17]

---

[12] Habel, *The Book of Job*, 534–35.
[13] Ibid., 540.
[14] Ibid., 542.
[15] Gutiérrez, *On Job*, 78.
[16] Ibid.
[17] Habel, *The Book of Job*, 544.

As Yahweh's speech progresses, Job becomes aware of his own place in the universe. In response to God's cosmic *'etsah*, Job replies in 40:4, "I feel my littleness: what reply shall I give?" With this statement, Job begins to reject his former anthropocentrism and accept the realization that God's *'etsah* is beyond Job's comprehension.[18] But still the theme of justice remains a pressing concern. God challenges Job to reverse God's judgment. According to Gutiérrez, this challenge amounts to Yahweh asking of Job, "Do you persist in staying locked into a world of easy explanations? Are you going to dispute my right to control what comes upon you? Are you trying to imprison my free and gratuitous love in your theological concepts?"[19]

For Gutiérrez, this is the crucial point at which the God of liberation is recognized. God has expressed desire for *mishpat* (40:8), but God will not impose justice on human freedom. We, like Job, must first release God from our conceptions of justice, allowing *mishpat* to unfold as God intends, not as we imagine it should. When we have acknowledged our place, paradoxically we are released to participate in the process of justice. Yahweh stops at the threshold of human freedom to "ask for their collaboration in the building of the world and in its just governance."[20]

Yahweh's speeches not only provide assurance for Job but also show how Job is a participant in the unfolding of justice. When faced with confounding pain and injustice, we can trust in this processive justice, knowing all the while that we are bound in Yahweh's *'etsah* and love. What good news this appears to be to Gutiérrez! He recounts the prayer of murdered Bolivian priest Luis Espinal, words that could be read with equal profundity by the people of Ayacucho:

> Train us, Lord, to fling ourselves upon the impossible,
> for behind the impossible is your grace and your presence;
> we cannot fall into emptiness.
> The future is an enigma,
> our road is covered by mist,
> but we want to go on giving ourselves,

---

[18] Gutiérrez, *On Job*, 76.
[19] Ibid., 77.
[20] Ibid., 79.

>because you continue hoping amid the night
>and weeping tears through a thousand human eyes."[21]

Job teaches us to speak loudly of injustice, while resting in the assurance of God's gratuitous love and wondrous *'etsah*. From this place we are released to fling ourselves on the impossible and participate in the unfolding of justice.

---

[21] Ibid., 91.

Chapter 9

Relinquishing illusions, finding joy
Ecclesiastes 11:1–8

Gloria Beck

The book of Qoheleth is written in the form of sayings collections and first-person observations.[1] Following the pattern of other ancient literature of its time, the author makes a notable person the primary voice through whom to tell the story and instruct the audience. He has selected one of Israel's most famous kings, Solomon, who is apparently at the end of his life, facing death.[2] But in a departure from earlier wisdom, Qoheleth questions trust in a God who rewards good and punishes evil. A common theme pointing to the meaninglessness of life runs through the book and is apparent in its thirty-eight uses of the word *hevel* ("vanity"). Another way to look at this theme might be as a lament that life has passed by too quickly for the writer.[3] As he looks back on his life, he struggles to find meaning.

It is not just the fact of physical death that disturbs Qoheleth; it is also the lack of human understanding of God's ways.[4] The life experiences of the writer have undermined the conviction that God always intends good things for devout people and punishes the rest. Like Job, Qoheleth abandons this view of God.[5] Throughout the book, Qoheleth seems to be trying to free God from the limits human understanding seeks to place on the divine.[6] But at the same time,

---

Gloria Beck is a member of Lockport Mennonite Church, Stryker, Ohio. Job and Wisdom Literature was her first seminary class.

[1] Leo G. Perdue, *Wisdom and Creation: The Theology of Wisdom Literature* (Nashville: Abingdon Press, 1994), 194.
[2] Ibid., 202.
[3] Ibid., 206–7.
[4] Kathleen M. O'Connor, *The Wisdom Literature,* Message of Biblical Spirituality 5 (Wilmington, DE: Michael Glazier, 1988), 114.
[5] James L. Crenshaw, *Old Testament Wisdom: An Introduction* (Louisville: Westminster John Knox Press, 1998), 117–18.
[6] O'Connor, *The Wisdom Literature,* 126.

he struggles with the knowledge that he cannot understand God's ways and is left feeling hopeless and unable to control the future. This sense of relinquishing the illusion that we possess knowledge and control is especially true of Ecclesiastes 11:1-8.

> [1]Send out your bread upon the waters,
>   for after many days you will get it back.
> [2]Divide your means seven ways, or even eight,
>   for you do not know
>   what disaster may happen on earth.
> [3]When clouds are full,
>   they empty rain on the earth;
> whether a tree falls to the south or to the north,
>   in the place where the tree falls, there it will lie.
> [4]Whoever observes the wind will not sow;
>   and whoever regards the clouds will not reap.
>
> [5]Just as you do not know how the breath comes to the bones in the mother's womb, so you do not know the work of God, who makes everything.
>
> [6]In the morning sow your seed, and at evening do not let your hands be idle; for you do not know which will prosper, this or that, or whether both alike will be good.
>
> [7]Light is sweet, and it is pleasant for the eyes to see the sun.
>
> [8]Even those who live many years should rejoice in them all; yet let them remember that the days of darkness will be many. All that comes is vanity.

Four times the idea of not knowing emerges in these verses. The first "do not know" comes in the form of a gentle reproof. "Send out your bread upon the waters" seems to be a call to be generous with those in need, "for you do not know what disaster might happen on the earth." We are to be so generous in our giving that our liberality might, to human understanding, seem like risky business, like throwing our resources away. The means mentioned in verse two might refer not only to wealth but also to our time or our talents.[7]

---

[7] Michael V. Fox, *Qohelet and His Contradictions* (Decatur, GA: The Almond Press, 1989), 273.

We should risk charity from whatever abundance we find ourselves in. Just as clouds give from their abundance or fullness to benefit the earth below, so we should give from the fullness of our abundance to benefit those around us. This proverb seems to manifest a sense of urgency about taking advantage of our opportunities while we have them. When the tree has been uprooted, when death comes, we will no longer have the ability to affect anything.

Qoheleth compares his understanding of the meaning of life with his understanding of the wind. There is little question that the wind exists, but humans do not understand its beginning or its end. It can appear without warning, touch our cheek, and then disappear.

The writer seems to be leading the reader into a thought process that removes from human hands any control of the future. He continues with the second and third occurrences of "do not know" in this passage. Just as we do not know how breath or life or the spirit comes to a developing fetus, we do not know or understand the divine mystery of the work of God. The miracle of life occurs, and no one knows how such a transformation takes place; likewise, God moves within the universe, and we are often clueless about the times of divine presence.[8] And finally, because we do not understand the work of God, we do not know which things will prosper and which will not. Clouds empty rain, trees fall, and a fetus is formed—and all are beyond human understanding.

While not abandoning wisdom altogether, the writer points out that the pursuit of wisdom is limited in a world that seems to be run by divine fate. The reader is counseled to submit to the reality of divine sovereignty. We are reminded that humanity is not the center of the universe. God—not humanity—rules, in what appears to be utter secrecy. Failure to accept God's rule and our human limitations in understanding could cost us the one divine gift awarded to those who please God. It is, the writer concedes, a gift that may actually make life worthwhile and meaningful. This gift is joy.[9]

So then, how are we to live? Life seems to the writer to be most meaningful when it is lived in simplicity. In youth or age, in all seasons, we are to do whatever God gives us to do, daily finding

---

[8] Crenshaw, *Old Testament Wisdom*, 123.
[9] Perdue, *Wisdom and Creation*, 237–42.

joy in the work before us. Just as clouds benefit the earth when they empty rain, so our generosity in sharing our means will benefit others. Pleasure is to be found in each day we are given life: in the work we do, the food we eat, and our relationships with those around us. At the heart of Qoheleth's message is appreciation for the fact that life is primarily for living, and every other human endeavor holds a secondary place. All toil, all progress, and all organization have merit to the extent that they promote and enhance living.[10] The Creator has made living an exciting adventure and has planted the capacity for happiness in the human heart,[11] so Qoheleth urges us: Do not let fear of disaster lead you to refuse to live and enjoy life. Take risks. We do not know what surprises might come our way. Life, both the good and the bad, should be lived intensely. In so living, we please God.

This counsel to enjoy and celebrate life itself seems to be the value Qoheleth has found in living and the thing he most wants to pass on. A life filled with joy is worth living.

---

[10] Dianne Bergant, *Israel's Wisdom Literature: A Liberation-Critical Reading* (Minneapolis: Fortress Press, 1997), 121.
[11] Ibid., 122.

Chapter 10

Because God is your share in life
A reading of Ecclesiastes 9:7–12

Suella Gerber

Ecclesiastes 9:7–12 re-presents the recurring theme in Qoheleth that the nature and meaning of this life are elusive.

⁷Go, eat your food with joy and drink your wine with a joyful heart because already God was pleased with your doings. ⁸In every time, let your clothes be clean and your head never without oil. ⁹And know life with a mate whom you love all the fleeting days of your lifetime which [God] gave to you beneath the sun, all your short-lived days because [God] is your share in life and in your effort as you work beneath the sun. ¹⁰All that your hand finds to do, do with your power, because there is no work or account or knowledge or wisdom in Sheol, where you are going.

¹¹And again I have seen beneath the sun that the running is not about the quick, or the battle about the mighty, or the food about the wise, or wealth about the discerning, or even favor about the knowing, because time and chance happen to all of them. ¹²Moreover, a person doesn't even know his or her time, like the fish that are caught in a miserable net or like the birds that are caught in the bird trap. Like these which are trapped are children of humanity in a time of crisis, when it falls on them suddenly.[1]

Throughout the book of Ecclesiastes, the writer dismantles conventional assumptions about life: the ways we think life should be, the things we think should or shouldn't happen. After each

---

Suella Gerber is a second-year student in the Master of Divinity program at Associated Mennonite Biblical Seminary. She is a member of Eighth Street Mennonite Church, Goshen, Indiana. John, her husband, is a teacher. They have two young adult children.

[1] Author's translation.

discussion on what life isn't, the writer responds with a version of "Life is elusive; live fully in the time that is given and known." This back and forth creates a rhythm that continues throughout the book; these reflections on Ecclesiastes 9:7–12 consider several beats of this rhythm.

Chapter 9 begins with a list of dualisms, noting that in life the things we assume are good or bad don't matter, because it all ends in death. Verses 7–10 are a response, commending a way to live in the face of that reality. And it begins with the fundamentals, with eating and drinking. "Go, eat your food with joy and drink your wine with a joyful heart, because already God was pleased with your doings." These three imperatives—go and eat and drink—aren't about eating and drinking for survival and sustenance, but the commands fit within a quality of life reflected in joy, gladness, and a heart that is pleased. This joy isn't a surface emotion; it infuses our entire being, with hints of feasting and celebrating with a community.

The second part of verse 7 gives the source of this joy: God has been pleased with what we've done. The verb is in the past tense, identifying a completed action. But if that isn't enough, the writer adds "already" to the verb. God has already found us favorable; God has already accepted us; God already was pleased. Knowing this, we can eat with joy and drink with joyful hearts. We don't need to be concerned with winning favor, with doing the right thing, but instead are free to live in the joy of knowing whose we are. There is no waiting for something in the future, since we may not even have the future. The joy is now, in this present moment.

Additional instructions follow in verse 8: "In every time, let your clothes be clean and your head never without oil." "In every time" may not be our typical way of speaking, but we miss something by translating this phrase as "always." "In every time" recalls the opening litany of chapter 3. The instruction is to wear clean clothes and have an oiled head in any circumstance, in all seasons. Just as the eating and drinking aren't about sustenance, this instruction is about more than personal hygiene. "Clean" clothes could also be translated as "white" clothes or "pure" clothes, adjectives suggesting elements of the festive and a pleasing offering. Likewise, the oil signals wealth, prosperity, and well-being, with echoes of anointing and ritual. European-Americans in the U.S. may not want to wear oil on their heads, but in a different climate with different hair, oil on one's head is restoring and refreshing. "Treat yourself with care and respect, no matter what circumstance you find yourself in." Although the Divine has already been pleased with what we have done, the approval isn't a blank check for any kind of behavior. How we eat and drink, how we present ourselves—in life, to God—requires celebration, joy, and preparation. Not just any behavior will do.

After addressing what we take into our bodies and how we present our bodies, the writer moves to companionship: "And know life with a mate whom you love all the fleeting days of your lifetime." I've translated this as "with a mate whom you love," rather than the literal "with a woman" or "with a wife," assuming the intention of this instruction isn't gender specific. Some modern interpreters wonder why the writer didn't use the definite article, "*the* woman" or "*the* wife." Within this discussion of life's *hevel*-ity,[2] I find irony in the so-human concern that the writer may not be supporting the institution of marriage! The issue here isn't marriage or promiscuity but rather that the enjoyment and fulfillment of life are meant to be shared, that giving and receiving love are essential.

Verse 9 continues, after this instruction: "And know life with a mate whom you love all the fleeting days of your lifetime, which [God] gave to you beneath the sun, all your short-lived days, because [God] is your share in life and in your effort as you work beneath the sun." The second part of this verse is most interesting: "because [God] is your share in life." It is also the place where my translation differs most from other translations. The *Tanakh* translates, "for that alone is what you can get out of life," and the NRSV, "because that is your portion in life." The difference in question is the independent third masculine singular pronoun, *hu'*, which I have translated as "he" or "God," and others have translated as "that." The difference in pronouns marks a significant difference in meaning. If life is *hevel* and God is our share, then God is what we have; God as our share gives us the means to eat and drink with joy, to present ourselves clean and restored in any circumstance, and to share life with loved ones. God as our share provides us with the purpose for getting out of bed every morning and going to work; it is for the Eternal that we toil under the sun.

---

[2] *Hevel* is the Hebrew word usually translated "vanity."

This paragraph concludes with verse 10's instruction on what we are to do. We are fed, we are ready, we are loved and share love, and we have our purpose. Now it is time to act: "All that your hand finds to do, do with your power, because there is no work or account or knowledge or wisdom in Sheol, where you are going." "Do with your power" is another imperative. The sense here is: Anything you do, everything you do, do with your strength and your full capacity. Don't be lukewarm or halfhearted. Give life everything you've got, because when you die, none of this matters. The things we assume are important are not only unimportant in Sheol, they are nonexistent there. What matters in life is not what we accomplish or accumulate or know; what matters is our being in our living.

As he begins a new paragraph, the writer begins a new repetition of his recurring patterns, challenging our assumptions, this time about winning and wealth and knowledge: "And again I have seen beneath the sun that the running is not about the quick, or the battle about the mighty, or the food about the wise, or wealth about the discerning, or even favor about the knowing, because time and chance happen to all of them." In this listing, the relationship between acts and results is debunked. At one level, the writer is saying that just because you're strong and fast, you won't necessarily win the race. But more than that, the point isn't winning or losing. Running is about running, with your strength and capacity, with what you've been given, at all times. And wisdom doesn't guarantee food. This wisdom isn't only in knowing how life works in the big picture. It's also a matter of having the skills and the experience of how life works, in a practical sense.

What is implied here is that just knowing how to work for food or how to earn a living doesn't yield food. Even more, food isn't the object of our wisdom; wisdom is the object of wisdom. The same is true for the other three pairs of this list: wealth and intelligence or discernment are not in a cause-and-effect relationship; strength and might don't mean winning wars; and favor and approval aren't the result of learning and knowing. Life isn't about expected results, "because time and chance happen to all of them." If you win the race and you're fast, great. But be clear that the winning is by chance, not necessarily a result of your speed!

But the writer of Ecclesiastes hasn't finished with this round. Verse 12 continues: "Moreover, a person doesn't even know his or her time, like the fish that are caught in a miserable net or like the birds that are caught in the bird trap. Like these which are trapped are children of humanity in a time of crisis, when it falls on them suddenly." We not only can't control the results of our efforts and abilities, we don't know what is going to happen to us. Not knowing our time isn't a matter of not knowing when we'll die; it's about not knowing the seasons of our lives, the events, the stages. It is in this sense that we are like fish in a net or birds in a snare. Crisis can occur at any time, and when it happens, we are caught and held by it.

The writer goes on to dismantle a new set of assumptions. If we read verses 11 and 12 in isolation, they are not good news; they're disheartening. To have our lives compared to trapped birds is cause to be discouraged. But read as a unit, these six verses are good news! Read as a unit, we see that when we are in crisis, we don't need to be victims. If these were the only verses in the book, the message could be complete. With these verses, the writer upsets the beliefs that most of us live by; he empties us of the things we have believed to be true. We cannot be filled with wisdom if we are full of human knowing. We cannot be filled if we are not empty first.

But there is also a practical benefit of heeding these commands. When the Divine is at the center of our lives, when that presence is what we have and hold, when we live in joy at all times, when we live loving others and knowing we're loved, when we live giving everything we've got, then it doesn't really matter what happens. Anything can happen at any time and we may be in great pain, but we have the Eternal and we drink and wear clean clothes and love, because that is all there is to do. Our meaning and purpose don't depend on what happens. Our routines and practices are the same, whether or not we are in crisis. In misfortune we eat and drink with joy; in disaster we put oil on our heads; in adversity we love. Echoes of these instructions can be heard in Jesus's teachings, whether in the Beatitudes, or in his teachings about tomorrow, or in his own living with complete disregard for the standards and expectations of the status quo.

Works consulted

Barton, George Aaron. *A Critical and Exegetical Commentary on the Book of Ecclesiastes*. The International Critical Commentary 17. Edinburgh: T & T Clark, 1947.

Brown, William P. *Ecclesiastes*. Interpretation: A Bible Commentary for Teaching and Preaching. Louisville: John Knox Press, 2000.

Clifford, Richard J., et al. *Introduction to Wisdom Literature, the Book of Proverbs, the Book of Ecclesiastes, the Song of Songs, the Book of Wisdom, the Book of Sirach.* The New Interpreter's Bible 5. Nashville: Abingdon Press, 1997.

Krüger, Thomas, et al. *Qoheleth*. Hermeneia—A Critical and Historical Commentary on the Bible. Minneapolis: Fortress Press, 2004.

Limburg, James. *Encountering Ecclesiastes: A Book for Our Time*. Grand Rapids: Eerdmans, 2006.

O'Connor, Kathleen M. *The Wisdom Literature*. Message of Biblical Spirituality 5. Wilmington, DE.: Michael Glazier, 1988.

Shields, Martin A. *The End of Wisdom: A Reappraisal of the Historical and Canonical Function of Ecclesiastes.* Winona Lake, IN: Eisenbrauns, 2006.

Chapter 11

Paradoxes and contradictions in Ecclesiastes 7:1–18

Sylvie Gudin

At first glance, Ecclesiastes 7:1–18 seems to consist of proverbs of traditional wisdom. But a closer look yields a different impression: the content of these verses tends to deny traditional wisdom statements, either by subtle shifts of perspective or by direct opposition. Even the form of the discourse reflects a realist's tearing up of conventional ideas; gradually bits of prose appear within the chain of proverbs.

Qoheleth, the author of Ecclesiastes, sees paradoxes in the truths he discovers. He recognizes the contradictions of life; they are evidence for his claim that "everything is vanity." "Qoheleth uses contradictions as the lens through which to view life," writes Michael Fox in *Qohelet and His Contradictions*.[1] Qoheleth himself seems to be full of contradictions: he appears to be pious, skeptical, pessimistic, and hedonistic—all at the same time! In this he is utterly human.

The contradictions and paradoxes in his writing do not indicate that the author's thinking is chaotic. On the contrary, his thought reveals a deep logic which has inspired many modern philosophers. The philosophy of existentialism, as developed by Jean-Paul Sartre, and the philosophy of absurdism, associated with Albert Camus, bear striking similarities to Ecclesiastes' philosophy. Qoheleth sees the world as *hevel*, which is usually translated as "vanity" but which could well be translated "absurdity." Camus describes the

---

Sylvie Gudin is studying at Associated Mennonite Biblical Seminary in the Master of Arts in Christian Formation program, with an emphasis on Christian spirituality. Originally from France, Sylvie also does translation work for Mennonite World Conference. She worships with Fellowship of Hope in Elkhart, Indiana.

[1] Michael Fox, *Qohelet and His Contradictions* (Decatur, GA: The Almond Press, 1989), 11.

human condition as absurd. "The essence of the absurd is a disparity between two phenomena that are supposed to be joined by a link of harmony or causality, but are actually disjunctive or even conflicting. The absurd is irrational, an affront to reason, in the broad sense of the human faculty that seeks and discovers order in the world about us."[2] Isn't this depiction of the absurd an apt description of the way Qoheleth views the world?

In Ecclesiastes 7:1–18, this sense of the absurd is especially striking, in spite of Qoheleth's logical thought process. In the last verse of the preceding chapter (6:12), he asks the rhetorical question, "Who knows what is good for mortals while they live the few days of their vain life?" Chapter 7 is an attempt to ponder this question—and offer some hints rather than definite answers.

Two themes dominate and unify the section: memento mori (life/death and sorrow/joy) and carpe diem (wisdom/folly). Unity is provided by the repetition of words: words of the same semantic field, words associated with pleasure and their antonyms, and words associated with displeasure.

Memento mori (life/death and sorrow/joy)

The first part of chapter 7 of Job (vv. 1–12) comprises proverbs constructed on the "better than" pattern. Although this construction is found throughout the Bible, it is especially characteristic of Wisdom literature. It appears in other parts of Ecclesiastes (4:2–3, for example), but the early verses of chapter 7 are the longest sequence of "better than" in the whole Bible.

This "better than" formula has a pedagogical function. A teacher can use it to make learning more engaging and as an aid to memorization. On a deeper level, these "better than" verses are significant in light of Qoheleth's philosophy. The repetition of "better than" indicates that, unlike much traditional wisdom, Qoheleth does not see the world in a dualistic way (good versus bad or wrong). Rather, he states that nothing is absolutely good or absolutely bad or wrong. But some things are better than others. Values are relative. When one understands that conviction, the writings of Qoheleth make sense. He acknowledges that the world has an element of the absurd, but still we can deal with it. We can find a way of life that does not lead us to despair. It is even possible

---

[2] Ibid., 31.

to enjoy life, because if we cannot know for sure what is good, at least wisdom can help us know what is better.

Some of these values are common in Wisdom literature (see vv. 1a, 5a, 9). Others intend to unsettle the reader comfortable with wisdom orthodoxy (see vv. 1b, 2, 3, 11). Let us study the statements about life and death.

From the beginning, in verse 1, the reader learns that Qoheleth intends to shock. The first proverbs use striking oppositions and parallelism. And not only that, but they seem to reverse ordinary insight. Is "the day of death" really better than "the day of birth"? Usually people rejoice at the birth of a baby and lament when someone dies. We find a parallel opposition in the next verse: "It is better to go to the house of mourning than to go to the house of feasting." And verse 3 continues in the same vein: "Sorrow is better than laughter." But given the choice, who would prefer to cry rather than laugh?

I see two levels of contradictions and paradoxes: first, in the fact that life leading only to death makes life a vanity or an absurdity; and second, in the fact that what Qoheleth describes as better would probably be what most people would think is worse.

There are hints at some explanation. Already in verse 2, Qoheleth warns us to live in the light of death, to remember that we must die. We should be present at funerals because we might learn something about our own mortality. The rituals that surround death remind us that we have been given the gift of life for a limited time only. Verse 4 offers us a key: "The heart of the wise is in the house of mourning." Here we learn that we are not so much dealing with facts of life as with perspective on life, which is one definition of wisdom.

Another common theme in Qoheleth's philosophy is the awareness that uncertainty is difficult for humans to endure. What makes the end better than the beginning? Then, we know; we are no longer in doubt about how a thing will end. Qoheleth expresses relief that life has an end, that finally it will be over and we can escape from life's oppression and meaninglessness.

Carpe diem (wisdom/folly)

What is wisdom according to Qoheleth, then? It seems to be a pretty dreary object. Remember the end of the first chapter? "For in much wisdom is much vexation, and those who increase knowledge increase sorrow" (1:18). We know right at the beginning of Ecclesiastes what we are in for: vexation and sorrow! These two themes, wisdom and grief, are interrelated. At the same time (another paradox), "wisdom gives life to the ones who possesses it" (v. 12). Qoheleth's concept of wisdom needs to be explored: How can pain and death be better than joy and life, especially if wisdom herself gives life?

What Qoheleth finds better is for human beings to be aware of and lucid about the limitations of human life. "Do not entertain illusions about what life is about," he tells us. We humans are not God. We have critical limitations, death being the obvious—ultimate—one, and our ignorance of the future is another definite one (v. 14). To be wise is to live in the recognition that we will eventually die. This awareness leads us to appreciate the days of our life; their brevity emphasizes their preciousness. Looking at life this way tends to help us treasure and enjoy each day.

Still, enjoying is not synonymous with feasting, which can be associated with drinking. This is a possible understanding of verse 3, which states that a "sad face/countenance" makes the heart "wiser" or "glad" (depending on the translation). Joy can be hollow; it can be "the laughter of fools," which is vanity, or absurd. Qoheleth underlines the superiority of gravity and sobriety over hilarity and fun, which are associated with folly. Wisdom and sobriety go together as do folly and mirth.

This is the reason a rebuke is instructive when it comes from a wise man (v. 5), or from God, as a form of discipline. One of these helpful rebukes is, for example, the pragmatic warning against idealizing the good old days: do not to live in the past (v. 10).

The proverbs part of chapter 7, begun with a poem that reads as if it could have been drawn from traditional wisdom, ends with a comment that turns the usual logic inside out: "Consider the work of God: who can make straight what he has made crooked?" (v. 14). Crookedness and deviousness are elsewhere so consistently associated with evil and the wicked that it is startling to find them associated with God here. That is another paradox of life. If God makes all the days, he makes bad days, so we had better accept life as it comes and take the bad with the good. There is a dimension of fatalism in Qoheleth's philosophy, because wisdom and righteousness are limited (vv. 16–17), as well as vulnerable (v. 7): the truth of a wise man's words can be undermined by lust for wealth and by oppression. Also, the empirical observation of v. 15—"I have seen"—appears frequently in the book and usually introduces sad observations, of good people suffering and evil people thriving. These seem to indicate that the author disagrees with the wisdom of the ancient world, which held that God rewards the good and punishes the wicked.

Conclusion

The contradictions and paradoxes that Qoheleth underlines in this passage are a demonstration of the complexity of life: to different situations, different responses. Other wisdom books mention this aspect of the condition of human beings, but Ecclesiastes analyzes them with a rare depth. The world is incomprehensible to Qoheleth, and to humans, because God has deliberately designed things so that we remain in ignorance (v. 14).

Humans are capable of some wisdom, but perfection is beyond their reach. "Do not be too righteous": Qoheleth uses irony to state that excess—even in the area of wisdom—is not a good thing, because it could become an obsession. Given this state of things, the best people can do is to try to acquire the wisdom available and enjoy life while it lasts, especially "in the days of prosperity." Writing with a subtlety and nuance that encourages us to live our lives fully, facing both good and ill, Qoheleth helps us find a paradoxically off-balance balance in life.

Chapter 12

Living life in the present
Ecclesiastes 9:7-12

Jill Schreiber

⁷Go, eat your bread with enjoyment, and drink your wine with a merry heart; for God has long ago approved what you do. ⁸Let your garments always be white; do not let oil be lacking on your head. ⁹Enjoy life with the wife whom you love, all the days of your vain life that are given you under the sun, because that is your portion in life and in your toil at which you toil under the sun. ¹⁰Whatever your hand finds to do, do with your might; for there is no work or thought or knowledge or wisdom in Sheol, to which you are going.

¹¹Again I saw that under the sun the race is not to the swift, nor the battle to the strong, nor bread to the wise, nor riches to the intelligent, nor favor to the skillful; but time and chance happen to them all. ¹²For no one can anticipate the time of disaster. Like fish taken in a cruel net, and like birds caught in a snare, so mortals are snared at a time of calamity, when it suddenly falls upon them.

As I begin these reflections on Ecclesiastes 9:7-12, the darkness that comes with death seems all too imminent. My husband is in Fort Wayne searching for a friend, a good friend, the best man from our wedding. This friend has been missing since Easter Sunday. He is single, in constant physical pain from a back injury, and he has been unable to find work. He recently got an eviction notice. In the past, he has sometimes been suicidal. Dan

---

Jill Schreiber is studying at Associated Mennonite Biblical Seminary in the Master of Arts: Theological Studies program, with a concentration in theology and ethics. She is a member of First Mennonite Church, Urbana, Illinois. When she wrote this essay she was a full-time student at AMBS. She is now in a PhD program in social work, with plans to continue AMBS studies with occasional classes. She and Dan, her husband, have three children.

went to Fort Wayne on Thursday and has been searching hospitals and shelters for homeless people, and he has filed a missing person report with the police. I don't know what will happen if our friend is found dead. I also don't know what will happen if he is found alive.

It is with this awareness of death that I hear the words of Ecclesiastes 9:1–6, the verses that precede my chosen text (9:7–12). Many commentaries on Ecclesiastes group verses 7–10 with the first six verses of the chapter. In order to address verses 7–12, then, we need to have some sense of what precedes them. Attention to this context is especially important, given that the first six verses of chapter 9 are dark, in stark contrast to verses 7–10, which are upbeat.

When we consider Ecclesiastes 9:1–6 in larger context, we are left with a sense of life enjoyed under the shadow of death. According to commentator James Crenshaw, "A lengthening shadow extends throughout the book, becoming especially dark in this unit."[1] Chapter 9 does indeed begin with a sense of foreboding. Everyone dies, the righteous and unrighteous, sinners and people who swear oaths. "The hearts of all are full of evil; madness is in their hearts while they live, and after that they go to the dead" (v. 3). A sense of hopelessness pervades these verses.[2]

The mood shifts in verses 7–10. Here is the first use of the imperative in Ecclesiastes, in a clear instruction. Grammatically, the imperative form adds emphasis. Earlier in Ecclesiastes, Qoheleth states that "it is fitting to eat and drink and find enjoyment in all the toil with which one toils under the sun" (5:18). In 9:7 the same sentiment appears, but now recast as an instruction: "Eat your bread

---

[1] James Crenshaw, *Ecclesiastes* (Louisville: Westminster John Knox Press, 1987), 159.
[2] The first six verses also include the comment that a living dog is better than a dead lion, implying that any common animal that is living is better than the most majestic animal that is dead. This verse was quoted at the funeral of Mary Queen of Scots in front of Queen Elizabeth. It was perhaps not the most judicious text for a royal funeral; indeed, the sermon was labeled "explosive." Another more recent and less inflammatory use of the living dog/dead lion text appeared in the Peanuts comic strip. Charlie Brown questions the meaning of the phrase, and Snoopy replies, "I don't know but I agree with it" (Eric Christianson, *Ecclesiastes through the Centuries* [Malden, MA: Blackwell Publishing, 2007], 208–9). In reading Ecclesiastes, we often have the sense that the meaning of the text is unclear, foggy, or ethereal, but we like it anyway.

with enjoyment, and drink your wine with a merry heart." These are clear instructions about how to live life well.

In verses 7–9 Qoheleth is not suggesting that we take up hedonism, and in verse 10 he is not suggesting that we become workaholics. Verse 10 is often cited in movies and books, perhaps because it plays so well to Americans with our work ethic. The professional engineering fraternity Theta Tau, for example, has adopted as its motto, "Whatsoever thy hand findeth to do, do it with thy might."[3] But it is important that we see these instructions in the context in which the writer of Ecclesiastes presents them. On either side of the calls to eat, drink, make love, and love your work (verses 7–10) are strong calls to be aware that we all die and life is limited.

These instructions have parallels in instructions found in the popular ancient Near Eastern story of Gilgamesh, a fact that has prompted several commentators to postulate Qoheleth's exposure to the earlier piece of literature. These words of Gilgamesh have a similar ring: "Let your belly be full. Make every day a day of rejoicing. Dance and play every night. Let your raiment be clean. Let your wife rejoice in your breast, and cherish the little one holding your hand."[4]

Verse 10 ends with the reference to Sheol. When Ecclesiastes was written, people understood death as an endless sleep, a forever darkness. Not until Daniel 12 is a notion of an afterlife—including resurrection—introduced in Hebrew scriptures; Daniel was written after Ecclesiastes.[5] Given our post-resurrection view of the afterlife, do Qoheleth's words have any value for us today? He is instructing us to live fully, because nothing is left for us in death. Should we listen to him, if we believe that death is not an end?

I found relevance for these verses in a surprising context: the Enneagram. The Enneagram is a tool for describing different personalities and their strengths and weaknesses. It can be used to better understand oneself and others.

---

[3] Theta Tau describes itself as the oldest (founded 1904) and largest professional engineering fraternity in the United States; see http://www.schach.eu/theta_tau_en.html.
[4] Old Babylonian version (Sippar iii.1–14). I like the addition of cherishing the "little ones." I wonder why Qoheleth left that part out.
[5] John Collins, *Introduction to the Hebrew Bible* (Minneapolis: Fortress Press, 2004), 570.

Verses 7–10 in Ecclesiastes seem like a credo for healthy, high-functioning Sevens on the Enneagram scale. So it is no surprise that I was drawn to it, for I am a One.[6] Ones at their best function like healthy Sevens. Therefore this verse clearly speaks truth to me and inspires me to be my best self, let go of my over-idealistic dreams, my desire to achieve, my need to fix the world, and instead invites me to relax and enjoy it more. The following is a description of high-functioning Type Sevens.[7]

> **Level 1 (At Their Best):** Assimilate experiences in depth, making them deeply grateful and appreciative for what they have. Become awed by the simple wonders of life: joyous and ecstatic. Intimations of spiritual reality, of the boundless goodness of life.
>
> **Level 2:** Highly responsive, excitable, enthusiastic about sensation and experience. Most extroverted type: stimuli bring immediate responses—they find everything invigorating. Lively, vivacious, eager, spontaneous, resilient, cheerful.
>
> **Level 3:** Easily become accomplished achievers, generalists who do many different things well: multi-talented. Practical, productive, usually prolific, cross-fertilizing areas of interest.[8]

Eating and drinking with a merry heart, having sex with one's spouse, and dressing well are simple wonders in life. Assimilating experiences in depth and feeling appreciation for what one has are quintessentially Qoheleth approaches to life. The energy of the Enneagram Seven clearly corresponds with that of Ecclesiastes. This Bible passage can guide one and inform a way of living. I suspect that this one may be a good one for me, because it calls me out of my weaknesses and into areas of strength.

Furthermore, even though I do not have a belief in Sheol, I still believe and keep in awareness the conviction that death is an end of life as we know it. I am sure we need to be alive while we are

---

[6] I spent part of my spring break delving into the Ennegram. I was surprised to find connections between the Enneagram and my Ecclesiastes passage.

[7] See the Enneagram Institute Web page: http://www.enneagraminstitute.com/TypeSeven.asp.

[8] Note that there are nine levels and that I did not include average or low functioning descriptions of sevens.

alive and appreciate the gifts we are given. I try to hold these gifts loosely, for we never know what the future will bring.

Verses 11 and 12 do not refer directly to death but to "times of disaster," which surely encompass the possibility of death. There is a sense of randomness to God's responses to our actions. Even if we are intelligent, skillful, strong, and swift, disaster may fall on us. None of us is immune to calamity. Job should not be surprised that disaster after disaster struck, because we all are subject to chance.

Verse 11 is another Ecclesiastes text that has had a lot of recent coverage in the media: Perhaps the most famous use of the text was by George Orwell.[9] He wrote an essay, "Politics and the English Language," in 1946. In it, he criticizes "ugly and inaccurate" contemporary written English and asserts that it is both a cause and an effect of foolish thinking and dishonest politics. In making his case, he quotes Ecclesiastes 9:11. He uses it as an example of excellent writing and then translates it into modern English of the worst sort:

Original Translation

I returned and saw under the sun, that the race is not to the swift, nor the battle to the strong, neither yet bread to the wise, nor yet riches to men of understanding, nor yet favour to men of skill; but time and chance happeneth to them all.

Modern Translation

Objective considerations of contemporary phenomena compel the conclusion that success or failure in competitive activities exhibits no tendency to be commensurate with innate capacity, but that a considerable element of the unpredictable must invariably be taken into account.

Orwell developed six rules for good writing in order to prevent such travesties:

1. Never use a metaphor, simile, or other figure of speech which you are used to seeing in print.

---

[9] A less well-known reference is the title of the *Star Trek: Deep Space 9* episode, "Nor the Battle to the Strong," which was inspired by Eccles. 9:11.

2. Never use a long word where a short one will do.
3. If it is possible to cut a word out, always cut it out.
4. Never use the passive where you can use the active.
5. Never use a foreign phrase, a scientific word, or a jargon word if you can think of an everyday English equivalent.
6. Break any of these rules sooner than say anything outright barbarous.

The contemporary cultural relevance of Ecclesiastes is evident in the sheer number of modern references to it and in the diversity of the sources that still find its truths germane, from George Orwell to Charles Shultz, from the Enneagram to the engineering society, not to mention a *Deep Space Nine* episode. Among this variety of those who have found it to be relevant, I count myself one who has found great truth and direction for myself in these words of Qoheleth.

Thursday night we finally received word from our friend. He is alive, in Colorado, and checking himself into the Veterans' Administration hospital. We hope we can help him recover an appreciation of the value of life, so that he can again eat his bread with enjoyment and sense that God has long ago approved of what he has done. May we and he find words of wisdom as we seek the way to delight in life's good gifts.

Chapter 13

An Easter message?
Ecclesiastes 9:7–12

Rachel Siemens

⁷Go, eat your bread with enjoyment, and drink your wine with a merry heart; for God has long ago approved what you do. ⁸Let your garments always be white; do not let oil be lacking on your head. ⁹Enjoy life with the wife whom you love, all the days of your vain life that are given you under the sun, because that is your portion in life and in your toil at which you toil under the sun. ¹⁰Whatever your hand finds to do, do with your might; for there is no work or thought or knowledge or wisdom in Sheol, to which you are going.

¹¹Again I saw that under the sun the race is not to the swift, nor the battle to the strong, nor bread to the wise, nor riches to the intelligent, nor favor to the skillful; but time and chance happen to them all. ¹²For no one can anticipate the time of disaster. Like fish taken in a cruel net, and like birds caught in a snare, so mortals are snared at a time of calamity, when it suddenly falls upon them.

As I read these words of Qoheleth in light of the recent splendor of Easter, I was drawn in by the beauty of the imagery: white garments, abundant oil, enjoyment, a merry heart. The text begins with bread and wine, the Maundy Thursday elements; when combined, these two are more often associated with New Testament observances than with the Hebrew Bible. The message of the text is an exhortation to enjoy life, because death and disaster draw near. I wanted to rush in and make real these connections that were buzzing around in my mind. I wanted to claim these verses as Easter verses.

Rachel Siemens is pastor of First Mennonite Church in Wadsworth, Ohio. She graduated from Associated Mennonite Biblical Seminary in 2007 with a Master of Divinity degree.

But alas, that is not how we do exegetical work. I needed to lay aside what I wanted the text to say and listen to what the text actually says. In the pages that follow, I offer what I have discovered through working with this pericope, and suggest some ways we can appropriate its meaning in our time.

This unit may be divided into two sections: the first, verses 7-10, which I see as an exhortation, and the second, verses 11-12, a reason or explanation for the exhortation.

Most of what Qoheleth has to say in this section is not new to the reader of the book of Ecclesiastes thus far. We have heard the words before, as early as chapter 2: "There is nothing better for mortals than to eat and drink, and find enjoyment in their toil. This also, I saw, is from the hand of God; for apart from him who can eat or who can have enjoyment?" (2:24-25). Mortals are to eat, drink, make merry. We are to enjoy life. Better yet, we are to enjoy life with someone we love. There are echoes of 4:9-12 ("Two are better than one . . .") in the exhortation to "enjoy life with the wife [or woman] whom you love" (9:9).

The assertion that "life is vain under the sun" is also not news to one who has read Ecclesiastes thus far. Neither is the linking of toil with life. As Sibley Towner writes, "For Qoheleth, toil and life are practically identical."[1] We see the identification in the parallelism of this verse: "because that is your portion in life and in your toil at which you toil under the sun" (9:9). Towner also notes that throughout Ecclesiastes, the word *toil* carries with it negative connotations, and he makes the link between Qoheleth's use of the word and its use in Genesis 3, where toil is a consequence for Adam of having eaten the forbidden fruit. In this sense, toil is punishment. It is contrary to the way things are supposed to be. Work is blessing, but toil is curse—to toil is to "labor in vain."[2] According to William Brown, "Enjoyment has the power to redeem the notion of toil amid (rather than over and against) the vicissitudes of life, the elusiveness of gain, and the ravaging power of death."[3]

---

[1] W. Sibley Towner, "Ecclesiastes," in *Introduction to Wisdom Literature, the Book of Proverbs, the Book of Ecclesiastes, the Song of Songs, the Book of Wisdom, the Book of Sirach*, The New Interpreters Bible Commentary 5 (Nashville: Abingdon Press, 1995), 280.
[2] William P. Brown, "'Whatever Your Hand Finds to Do': Qoheleth's Work Ethic," *Interpretation* 55, no 3 (July 2001): 276.
[3] Ibid., 279.

Qoheleth is repeating himself here. The themes and words are familiar to us. Consideration of the recurring themes and terms of Ecclesiastes is a method of understanding the book, one Towner uses in the introduction to his commentary on Ecclesiastes. Instead of dividing the book structurally, he uses repeated words as a key to the book as a whole.[4] As I read through his list of key words, I started circling them in the text: *hevel* ("vain") occurs once; "life," three times; "toil," twice; "all," twice; *hokmah* ("wisdom"), twice, in different forms. A different noun is used for fate here, but the verb form of *miqreh* ("fate") is present.[5] Perhaps Qoheleth is reaching a climax, stopping to summarize all that he has previously said. Towner draws that conclusion.[6]

Not only are the central themes and terms of Qoheleth's message present in this text; here he treats them differently, in ways that seem to confirm that this text is the summary or climax of the book. Qoheleth's voice and tone change in this section. And he introduces new ideas and adds new images, images only found in this portion of the book.

The first change I noticed is the use of the imperative tense for the verbs. He is no longer content to observe that "there is nothing better for mortals . . ." Instead he uses direct address, framing commands for his hearers: Go. Eat. Drink. Celebrate. Enjoy. Do. These things that I have been telling you that humans should do, go out and do them. I am not engaged in mere philosophizing. These words are meant for you to act on! And this advice that Qoheleth gives, these admonitions, are universal in nature; most commentators highlight strong similarities between these verses and a section of the popular ancient Mesopotamian *Epic of Gilgamesh*, in which the tavern keeper Siduri gives Gilgamesh the same advice.[7]

A second phrase that stood out for me was this one: "for God has long ago approved what you do." God approves. God has long ago approved! God's approval is prior to our enjoyment. We had known that Qoheleth sees God's hand in human enjoyments, but here the observation moves up a notch: God has long ago approved

---

[4] Towner, "Ecclesiastes," 278–82.
[5] *Pena* is the noun for "fate."
[6] Towner, "Ecclesiastes," 339.
[7] See Milton P. Horne, *Proverbs, Ecclesiastes*, Smith & Helwys Bible Commentary (Macon, GA: Smith & Helwys Publishing, 2003), 501.

what you do. Roland Murphy comments on the use of the Hebrew verb *ratza* ("to be pleased"). "The verb is often used of divine pleasure in sacrifices."[8] God is often described in the Old Testament as given to harsh judgment, yet here is a God who takes pleasure in God's people. This divine enjoyment of humanity is an aspect of the divine character to which we need to pay more attention.

Next Qoheleth introduces new images of festivity and joy, complete with white garments and an abundance of oil. God delights in human enjoyment. Enjoy your work all your days, for there is no enjoyment in the place to which you are going. And with that, Qoheleth introduces Sheol. This is the only use of the name in the entire book. At the end of the exhortation, Qoheleth is contrasting life under the sun to non-life in Sheol.[9]

With this introduction of Sheol at the conclusion of this section, we are ready to move on to the next one: the reason for the exhortation. Life is not logical. Things do not happen as they should; "time and chance happen to . . . all." In fact, the time of disaster and calamity may suddenly fall on us, and we are helpless to anticipate it. Do these words represent a gloomy, pessimistic fatalism on Qoheleth's part? Or is he simply making an observation about life? How do these words fit with the fact that he has just commanded us to celebrate? Are these to be taken as words of encouragement or discouragement?

Mercedes García Bachmann, an Argentinean theologian, writes that verses 11–12 "situate us in the realization that things do not always result in what one would logically expect."[10] But if the world is not logical, can we really trust God? She responds affirmatively, because verse 7 says "we can trust God, and be sure that God has accepted our deeds."[11]

Bachmann then asks us to ponder the following: "What about considering that God is pleased with human beings who are happy in their life, and who do not act out of fear or reward, either be-

---

[8] Roland E. Murphy, *Ecclesiastes*, Word Biblical Commentary (Dallas: Word Books, 1992), 92. Murphy compares the use of *ratza* here to its use in Deut. 33:11 and Amos 5:22.
[9] Sheol is the "place of the dead" in the Old Testament. For more information, see Theodore J. Lewis, "Dead, Abode of the," in *Anchor Bible Dictionary* 2:101–5.
[10] Mercedes García Bachmann, "A Study of Qoheleth (Ecclesiastes) 9:1–12," *International Review of Mission* 91, no. 362 (July 2002): 389.
[11] Ibid., 390.

fore or after death, but out of happiness, out of gratitude for life, out of joy, out of good will?"[12] With this sentence she summarizes Qoheleth's wisdom and provides us with an attitude for living. This stance can be seen as an act of rebellion in a society that assesses people's worth by what they produce. When we enjoy life, we live counterculturally.

For Bachmann, this attitude is not an "anything goes" approach, but rather one that pushes us beyond ourselves. She sees it as a "way of being human, of affirming the human condition in times and circumstances in which [people] . . . were denied their humanity."[13] She is referring to the people who are neglected and ignored in our societies. These words from Qoheleth allow the "nobodies" to hear "that God rejoices in their works and wants them/us to rejoice in whatever little . . . makes humans more humane."[14]

Though this passage is not traditionally associated with Easter, it does point us to the resurrection hope found in being an Easter people. Qoheleth gives us guidance—wisdom, even—on how to live as an Easter people, a people who trust in the God who delights in us.

---

[12] Ibid.
[13] Ibid.
[14] Ibid.

www.ingramcontent.com/pod-product-compliance
Lightning Source LLC
Chambersburg PA
CBHW070325100426
42743CB00011B/2567